A PRACTICAL GUIDE TO HANDLING MOTOR INSURERS' BUREAU CLAIMS

London • Sydney • Portland, Oregon

A PRACTICAL GUIDE TO HANDLING MOTOR INSURERS' BUREAU CLAIMS

Nick Jervis

Judy Dawson

Cavendish
Publishing
Limited

London • Sydney • Portland, Oregon

First published in Great Britain 2002 by
Cavendish Publishing Limited, The Glass House,
Wharton Street, London WC1X 9PX, United Kingdom
Telephone: + 44 (0)20 7278 8000   Facsimile: + 44 (0)20 7278 8080
Email: info@cavendishpublishing.com
Website: www.cavendishpublishing.com

Published in the United States by Cavendish Publishing
c/o International Specialized Book Services,
5804 NE Hassalo Street, Portland,
Oregon 97213-3644, USA

Published in Australia by Cavendish Publishing (Australia) Pty Ltd
3/303 Barrenjoey Road, Newport, NSW 2106, Australia

British Library Cataloguing in Publication Data
Jervis, Nick
A practical guide to handling Motor Insurers' Bureau claims
1 Motor Insurers' Bureau 2 Liability for traffic accidents – Great Britain
3 Automobile insurance claims – Great Britain
4 Insurance, uninsured motorist – law and legislation – Great Britain
I Title II Dawson, Judy
346.4'1'0323

Library of Congress Cataloguing in Publication Data
Data available

ISBN 1-85941-753-1

1 3 5 7 9 10 8 6 4 2

Printed and bound in Great Britain

FOREWORD

This is a truly refreshing book – it takes the practitioner by the hand through the 1999 Uninsured Drivers Agreement, and in a straightforward easy to follow manner gives practical advice on exactly what to do to avoid the many pitfalls where the defendant is an uninsured driver and the MIB the only recourse.

This is an area of law where there are few, if any, established textbooks. In any event, the theory is not enough. All practitioners need to know how to navigate the Agreement, when to follow it and when to follow the amended Notes for Guidance.

The reader will undoubtedly find the precedent letters, case management tips and in particular, the claims register invaluable. The book is a superb example of 'best practice' when dealing with the MIB and if followed using the checklists and precedents provided, there can be no excuse for not getting everything right. The scope is enormous, every reader can draw on this combination of theory and practice, precedent and procedure. The sound knowledge of the writers in this field and obvious experience at the sharp end provides helpful tips for the inexperienced and experienced practitioner alike.

As a motor practitioner of many years, I cannot praise this book too highly and recommend it as essential reading for all who deal with the MIB.

Janet Tilley
Chairman
Motor Accident Solicitors Society[1]
Bristol

---

1   See Appendix F.

ACKNOWLEDGMENTS

Anyone who has written a legal book will know the time involved in the process. I could not have managed without the overwhelming love and support of my wife, Emma, and the unconditional love of my two children, Megan and Samuel.

Thanks also to all at David Gist solicitors, all at MASS (particularly 'Hinge' with her constant nagging, Janet and Ian), and Bernie.

Nick Jervis
David Gist Solicitors

With grateful thanks to all at Unity Street Chambers, in particular John Isherwood who has provided love, advice and support through thick and thin; also to my ever-patient and loving husband, Owen Rees, and with love to my beautiful daughter, Amy Elizabeth, whose early arrival ensured that publication was delayed long enough for her to get a mention!

Judy Dawson
Unity Street Chambers

HOW TO USE THIS GUIDE

CHAPTER SUMMARY

This highlights the content of each chapter in line format. Once you are familiar with the guide, this should enable you to remember what action is required at each stage of the case by running through the chapter summary, and ticking off the tick boxes.

DIARY ENTRIES

Details the suggested warning entries to be inserted into your case management system, whether manual or computer based. The purpose is to ensure that all of the notice requirements and time limits are complied with.

PRECEDENT LETTERS

Inserted to assist compliance with the notice requirements of the Agreements and to ensure that all relevant enclosures are included. Also to warn your clients of their obligations in pursuing a claim under the MIB Agreements.

CHECKLISTS

To assist you in the preparation of the cases, to ensure you have the necessary information and documentation on the file when it is needed to comply with the various notice requirements.

QUESTIONNAIRES

To ensure you raise the relevant questions with your clients to obtain the necessary information or documentation to pursue a claim against the MIB.

WEBSITE

www.mib-help.co.uk is a new website designed to be used as a source of MIB information, and for sharing information on all MIB related matters. It is intended to cover referrals to the Secretary of State and his responses, and decisions made by the MIB under the Agreements.

WARNING

The suggested letters, procedures and practices in this book are the authors' interpretations of the Uninsured and Untraced Drivers Agreements and how they believe they might be interpreted. However, the court, the MIB or the Secretary of State may interpret the Agreements in a different manner. This book is intended as a guide only.

CONTENTS

APPENDICES

PRECEDENT DOCUMENT INDEX

DOCUMENTS

1999 Uninsured Drivers Agreement

Document Reference	Description	Chapter Number
D1	MIB communication receipt form	3.2
D2	MIB claims register	3.2
D3	Standard form for completion after discussion meeting	5.5
D4	Draft particulars of claim	6.6
D5	Draft witness statement for an application for service by alternative method	6.6
D6	Record of fax to the MIB	6.6

LETTERS

1999 Uninsured Drivers Agreement

Letter Reference	Description	Chapter Number
L1	Letter to the MIB regarding reserved notice point	2.8
L2	First letter to the client dealing with relevant issues	4.3
L3	Letter for the client to forward to the driver	4.3
L4	Letter to the driver from the solicitor	4.3
L5	Letter to the police regarding failure to supply insurance policy details	4.3
L6	Letter to be sent with DVLA search form	4.3
L7	Letter to the registered keeper from the solicitor	4.3
L8	Letter to the police regarding the registered keeper's failure to provide details	4.3
L9	Letter to the driver from the solicitor to be sent at various intervals prior to the expiry of the limitation period	5.6
L10	Covering letter to the MIB enclosing application form and supporting documentation	5.6

Letter Reference	Description	Chapter Number
L11	Letter to the MIB requesting that it be added as a defendant and confirms other matters	5.6
L12	Letter to the court for issue of proceedings against the MIB	6.7
L13	Letter to the claimant advising of the issue of proceedings	6.7
L14	Letter serving proceedings on the defendant	6.7
L15	Letter to the MIB serving proceedings/notice of service/notice of intention to apply for judgment	6.7
L16	Letter to the MIB giving notice of personal service of proceedings	6.7
L17	Letter to the MIB giving notice of confirmation of service on the defendant	6.7
L18	Letter serving the particulars of claim on the defendant (to include the MIB if a defendant)	7.3
L19	Letter to the MIB giving notice of service of the particulars of claim	7.3
L20	Letter to the MIB giving notice of the filing of a defence	7.3
L21	Letter to the MIB serving the amended particulars of claim/documents to be served therewith	7.3
L22	Letter to the medical expert warning all reports/letters to be sent by fax	7.3
L23	Letter to the MIB providing notice of the trial date being fixed/notice of filing of the allocation/listing questionnaire, etc	7.3
L24	Letter to the court serving the allocation or listing questionnaire	7.3
L25	Letter to the Secretary of State to request a decision on the reasonableness of the MIB's request	7.3
L26	Letter to the MIB enclosing a copy of the letter to the Secretary of State requesting a decision on the reasonableness of the MIB's further information request	7.3
L27	Letter to the client enclosing the MIB assignment and agreement form	9.3

Letter Reference	Description	Chapter Number
L28	Letter to the MIB requesting confirmation that it has no interest in the case	11.4
L29	Letter to the insurer requesting confirmation that it is dealing with the claim as a Road Traffic Act insurer	11.4
L30	Letter to the MIB confirming it will not take issue on provision of an incorrect notice	11.4

1988 Uninsured Drivers Agreement

Letter Reference	Description	Chapter Number
L31	Letter to the client to forward to the other driver	12.6
L32	Letter from the solicitor requesting insurance details	12.6
L33	Letter to the MIB providing notice of intention to apply for judgment	12.6

1996 Untraced Drivers Agreement

Letter Reference	Description	Chapter Number
L34	Letter to the client following receipt of instructions	14.3
L35	Letter to the police reporting the incident	14.3
L36	Letter to the MIB lodging the Untraced Drivers Agreement application form	14.3
L37	Letter to the MIB appealing the decision	15.8
L38	Undertaking to be sent with the letter enclosing the appeal	15.8

CHECKLISTS

1999 Uninsured Drivers Agreement

Checklist Reference	Description	Chapter Number
CL1	Excluded vehicles list	2.7
CL2	Proper Notice checklist	5.7
CL3	1999 Uninsured Drivers Agreement Notice checklist	7.4

QUESTIONNAIRES

1999 Uninsured Drivers Agreement

Questionnaire Reference	Description	Chapter Number
Q1	MIB questionnaire	4.4

FORMS

1999 Uninsured Drivers Agreement

Questionnaire Reference	Description	Chapter Number
F1	Instructions to the enquiry agent to locate the insurer/identify the driver	1.7

TABLE OF CASES

TABLE OF LEGISLATION

STATUTES

STATUTORY INSTRUMENTS

TABLE OF DIRECTIVES

CHAPTER 1

CLAIMS AGAINST THE UNINSURED DRIVER: A BASIC OUTLINE

CHAPTER SUMMARY

1.1	**The history of the MIB**	☐
1.2	**Finding an insurer**	☐
1.2.1	Practical tips	☐
1.2.1.1	The Motor Insurance Database	☐
1.2.1.2	DVLA searches	☐
1.2.1.3	Telephone enquiries	☐
1.2.1.4	Internet enquiries	☐
1.2.1.5	Personal enquiries	☐
1.2.2	Driver uninsured but vehicle insured	☐
1.2.2.1	Procedural requirements	☐
1.3	**The Untraced Drivers Agreement**	☐
1.4	**The Criminal Injuries Compensation Scheme**	☐
1.5	**The Uninsured Drivers Agreements**	☐
1.5.1	The European Directives	☐
1.6	**The MIB organisation**	☐
1.6.1	Who's who at the MIB	☐
1.6.2	The MIB contact details	☐
1.7	**Forms**	☐
F1	Instructions to the enquiry agent to locate the insurer/ identify the driver	☐

1.1 THE HISTORY OF THE MIB

It has long been recognised that innocent victims of road traffic accidents should be compensated; in practical terms, judgments against the offending driver could rarely be satisfied by that person, particularly given the medical advances which have led to many more people surviving accidents but facing a lifetime of needing medical treatment and care. Initially, this problem was dealt with by the government introducing compulsory insurance for all drivers. However, it became increasingly obvious that, due to non-compliance with these provisions, an anomaly was created whereby an innocent victim could obtain no compensation at all because they had the misfortune of having been injured by a penniless uninsured or untraced driver. By an agreement between the insurance companies and the government in 1945, provision was made for the establishment of a fund to satisfy judgments in certain cases; in 1946, the Motor Insurers' Bureau (MIB) was born. Since that time, there have been various agreements dealing with untraced and uninsured drivers.

If the aim of the various agreements is to ensure that the innocent victim of an uninsured or untraced driver is placed in the same position as an innocent victim of an insured driver (and according to European Directives to which the UK government has agreed, that is the aim), then the agreements have significant failings. The MIB, 'a novel piece of extra-statutory machinery',[1] has consistently placed procedural hurdles in the way of innocent victims, and even in cases where it is accepted that there has been no prejudice caused to the MIB, has insisted on relying on minor procedural breaches (for instance, notices being served a couple of days late) in order to escape any liability to satisfy a judgment.

It is important that all claimant solicitors understand that the MIB has no common law liability to the claimant and the only way that such liability to satisfy the judgment arises is under the relevant Agreement. Thus, the court has no discretion to excuse any breach of a condition by the claimant and order the MIB to satisfy a judgment, even if the overriding objective and every principle of fairness dictates that it should. Further, there are certain exceptions and limitations imposed, particularly by the 1999 Uninsured Drivers Agreement, which prevent any compensation being awarded. Whilst the passenger who accepts a lift from an insured driver who he knows is drunk will recover the majority of his damages, if the drunk driver was (unbeknown to the passenger) uninsured, the passenger will recover nothing from the MIB.[2] Such compensation as may be awarded against the negligent driver may not always be paid in full by the MIB in any event; if the innocent victim is the beneficiary of a personal accident plan, which pays out in the event of an injury, the MIB can deduct such sums from the compensation it pays, notwithstanding the fact that the innocent victim of an insured driver would receive the full amount.

---

1   *Per* Sir Ralph Gibson in *Silverton v Goodall and MIB* [1997] PIQR 451.
2   See 2.4.2.4.

There are some circumstances in which, despite the fact that the driver was uninsured, an insurer rather than the MIB will have to satisfy the judgment; this places the claimant in a more advantageous position.

1.2   FINDING AN INSURER

1.2.1   Practical tips

Assuming that the driver does not provide insurance details despite requests,[3] other action should be taken to trace a potential insurer.

1.2.1.1   *The Motor Insurance Database*

Run by the MIB's sister company, the Motor Insurers' Information Centre, this Database is designed to comply with the requirements of the Fourth Motor Insurance Directive. It records details of all insurance policies, including the date in force and the vehicles covered. There is not yet direct access for solicitors,[4] although insurers do have access to the Database. A telephone call to the claimant's insurer (or driver's insurer if the claimant was the passenger) should be made to discover whether a search has been made and the results of such a search (or to request that such a search is made). The Database is not 'live'. Some records are not entered onto the Database until many weeks after the policy is written. Therefore, it may be necessary to request the insurer concerned to search the Database again a few weeks after the accident.

Solicitors should continue to argue for direct access to the Database to avoid unnecessary delay in injury claims.

1.2.1.2   *DVLA searches*

If an insurer is not initially located, the solicitor should carry out a search for the registered keeper of the vehicle; this may be a different person from the driver of the vehicle at the time of the accident. The registered keeper may hold insurance which will cover the driver under the terms of the policy, or under the terms of the Road Traffic Act 1988 (see 1.2.2).[5] Demands for insurance details pursuant to s 154 of the Road Traffic Act 1988 must then be made.[6]

---

3   See 4.1.2.

4   The proposed Fifth Insurance Directive provides, in its draft form, for direct access for victims of all accidents. The MIB may start allowing access before it is in force. Therefore, requests should be made to the Motor Insurers' Information Centre if no other search reveals an insurer.

5   Section 151(2)(b) of the Road Traffic Act 1988.

6   See 4.1.2 and 4.1.4.

1.2.1.3   Telephone enquiries

Any telephone numbers obtained at the scene of the accident should be called; it is important to spend time confirming the identity of the other driver (and the registered keeper if different) at the beginning of the claim, as well as attempting to obtain insurance details, as this will avoid the MIB arguing that the driver is actually untraced rather than uninsured.[7] Telephone calls to discover if there is insurance should be made at different times of the day, including after office hours.

To support any future application for service by an alternative method,[8] records of such attempted calls should be made and a letter should be sent in advance to the driver or registered keeper warning them that you will make the call at a certain time, to allow them every opportunity of being available when you call.

1.2.1.4   Internet enquiries

There are now many facilities available on the internet to locate people. **192.com** is the internet directory enquiries and is reasonably cheap. There are others available and they should be used at the beginning of a claim to attempt to locate the driver or registered keeper in order to make contact and to discover whether any insurance exists.

1.2.1.5   Personal enquiries

Form F1

Although an expensive method, if it is successful in locating the driver or registered keeper and leads to the production of insurance details, it will avoid a significant amount of delay and expense. Instruct an enquiry agent to investigate the address, location and any insurance details.[9]

1.2.2   Driver uninsured but vehicle insured

Under s 151 of the Road Traffic Act 1988, where a judgment is obtained relating to a liability required to be covered by a policy of insurance,[10] and that liability is covered by the terms of a policy, and judgment is obtained against the person insured under the policy *or it is a liability which would be covered if the policy insured all persons,* then the insurer has a duty to satisfy such a judgment.

---

7   See 4.1.1.

8   See 6.3.1.

9   See 1.7, form F1.

10   Namely, personal injury or death caused by the use of a vehicle on a road or other public place.

The important points to consider differ depending on whether it is a person insured under the terms of the policy, or it is an identified person covered as a result of the provisions of s 152 of the Road Traffic Act 1988. If the former, the insurer may be able to avoid satisfying the claim where the policy excludes the use of the vehicle in certain circumstances (see example (3) in the table below). If the latter, there is less opportunity for the insurer to avoid the claim.

Practical examples

Your client is injured by:	Remedy:
(1) Uninsured wife who was driving her husband's car to the shops; he is insured for social and domestic use.	Husband's insurer will have to satisfy the judgment (s 151(2)(b) of the Road Traffic Act 1988).
(2) Uninsured thief in a vehicle insured by Mr Bloggs for social and domestic use.	Mr Bloggs' insurer will have to satisfy judgment;[11] thieving has been held to be social and domestic use.
(3) Mr Bloggs who was using his car as a mini-cab although he had only insured it for social and domestic use.	Insurer would not have to satisfy the judgment and the claim would have to be directed to the MIB as liability was not covered.[12]
(4) Uninsured thief without a driving licence in a vehicle insured by Mr Bloggs, whose policy specifically excludes people without a full driving licence.	Insurer would have to satisfy the judgment; s 151(3) states that restrictions on persons by reference to the holding of a driving licence by the driver shall have no effect.
(5) Mr Bloggs, whose insurance company had cancelled his policy of insurance prior to the accident.	Assuming that the insurer had met the requirements under s 152(1)(c) of the Road Traffic Act 1988,[13] it would not have to meet the judgment and the claim should be directed against the MIB.

11 Section 151(2)(b) of the Road Traffic Act 1988.

12 In reality, the insurer may well agree to deal with the claim under agreements that the insurers have with the MIB; this would be a matter for the insurer. Initial enquiries should be made with the insurer and it should be requested to confirm whether it was prepared to deal with the claim. NB: if the insurer states that it is acting on behalf of the MIB (under the Domestic Regulations Agreement or its replacement, Article 75), it is still technically an MIB claim and all provisions of the Agreement apply and have to be complied with.

13 Ie, either before the accident, the insurer had recovered the certificate from Mr Bloggs or Mr Bloggs had made a statutory declaration that he had lost or destroyed it, or after the accident but within 14 days of the cancellation, the insurer had recovered the certificate from Mr Bloggs or obtained such a statutory declaration, or within 14 days of cancellation (before or after the accident), the insurer had commenced proceedings against Mr Bloggs in respect of failure to surrender the policy.

Your client is injured by:	Remedy:
(6) Mr Bloggs who was insured but had lied on his insurance form about previous motoring convictions, entitling his insurance company to avoid the policy.	Insurer can avoid payment provided that it obtains a declaration that it is entitled to avoid the policy either before the claim is issued or within three months of issue.[14]
(7) Mr Bloggs who was uninsured but borrowed his (insured) friend's car to deliberately run over your client on a pedestrian crossing due to a long-running neighbour dispute.	Insurer would still have to satisfy the judgment; intentional harm is still required to be covered under the compulsory insurance provisions.[15]
(8) Uninsured but identified thief, who stole Mr Bloggs' car and rammed it through a private security fence into an enclosed locked compound of your client and mistakenly ran over your client.	Neither the insurer of Mr Bloggs' car nor the MIB would have to satisfy the judgment as the accident did not occur on a road or other public place.[16]

See 11.1 and 11.1.1.

1.2.2.1 *Procedural requirements*

In order for the claimant to be able to enforce judgment against the s 151 insurer, the insurer must have been given notice of the bringing of proceedings either before or within seven days of commencement of proceedings.[17]

1.3 THE UNTRACED DRIVERS AGREEMENT

Just as the government (and latterly the EU) decided that the innocent victims of uninsured drivers should be compensated, a similar decision was reached by both bodies in respect of the innocent victims of untraced drivers – to deal with those injured by 'hit and run' accidents or accidents where the driver either refused to give his details or gave a false name and/or details and was never

---

14 Section 152(2); the insurer must give notice to the claimant of the declaration proceedings.
15 *Hardy v MIB* [1964] 2 QB 745.
16 See 2.4.4 and *Charlton v Fisher* [2001] 3 WLR 1435; [2001] 1 All ER (Comm) 769; [2001] PIQR 23.
17 Section 152(1)(a) and see *Wake v Wylie* [2001] RTR 20; [2001] PIQR 13, in which a letter from the claimant's solicitors sent 17 months prior to the issue of proceedings was held not to have constituted notice of proceedings and therefore the insurer did not have to satisfy the judgment.

found. Proceedings in these cases cannot be issued (as there is no defendant to issue against) and need to be dealt with under the 1996 Untraced Drivers Agreement. It is important to establish which type of Agreement applies. There is anecdotal evidence that the MIB has successfully argued, after the three year deadline for an application under the Untraced Drivers Agreement has expired in a particular case, that that Agreement, rather than the Uninsured Drivers Agreement then existing, was the correct Agreement to proceed under, as the lack of any contact with the named defendant suggested that the driver in question had in fact given false details and the defendant did not actually exist. It is therefore important to establish contact with the defendant at an early stage[18] or, in the event of any doubt, proceed under both Agreements simultaneously.

1.4   THE CRIMINAL INJURIES COMPENSATION SCHEME

Victims of road traffic accidents cannot claim injury under the Criminal Injuries Compensation Scheme where 'the injury is attributable to the use of a vehicle, except where the vehicle was used so as deliberately to inflict, or attempt to inflict, injury on any person'.[19] Thus, the defendant's subsequent conviction for dangerous driving will not assist the victim, unless it is found that the defendant deliberately drove into the victim in order to injure him.[20] Even if such a finding is made, it will be very rarely advisable for the victim to proceed under the Criminal Injuries Compensation Scheme unless neither an insurer nor the MIB would satisfy any judgment obtained against the defendant (which would arise if the act occurred on private land, for instance), as the compensation received from the civil courts would almost certainly be higher than that recovered under the Scheme, and the Criminal Injuries Compensation Authority would be entitled to deduct any damages recovered from the civil courts.

1.5   THE UNINSURED DRIVERS AGREEMENTS

As outlined above in 1.1, the government and latterly the EU have decided that innocent victims of uninsured motorists should recover compensation for their injuries. Since 1946, this has been achieved by the payment of unsatisfied judgments against uninsured defendants by the MIB.

---

18   See 4.1.1.
19   Paragraph 11 of the 1996 Criminal Injuries Compensation Scheme.
20   See *R v Criminal Injuries Compensation Authority ex p M (A Minor)* [2000] RTR 21; [1999] PIQR 195.

1.5.1   The European Directives

The European Union has issued four Uninsured Drivers Directives.[21] The First ensured that Member States put into place a compulsory insurance scheme – in fact, the UK had had such a scheme in place for many years. The Second reiterated this aim, and at para 4 stated that: 'Each Member State shall set up or authorise a body with the task of providing compensation, at least up to the limits of the insurance obligation for damage to property or personal injuries caused by an unidentified vehicle or a vehicle for which the insurance obligation provided for in paragraph 1 has not been satisfied.' The UK did not pass legislation to implement this Directive, but entered into a new agreement with its insurers, under the auspices of the MIB. The Third Directive required that insurance should extend to liability for personal injuries to all passengers arising out of the use of a motor vehicle, which was implemented by the Motor Vehicles (Compulsory Insurance) Regulations 1992. The Fourth Directive concerned claims which resulted from accidents in foreign countries and has led to the creation of the Motor Insurance Database.[22] The Fifth Directive is currently in the consultation process, but in its draft form allows for direct access to the Motor Insurance Database, removes the ability for the MIB to avoid liability if a passenger enters a car with a drunk driver and is subsequently injured, and will allow for recovery of property damage in untraced claims where the applicant suffers significant personal injuries.

---

21   72/166/EEC; 84/5/EEC; and 90/232/EEC.
22   See 1.2.1.1.

1.6   THE MIB ORGANISATION

1.6.1   Who's who at the MIB

James Read

A former solicitor who is now the chief executive of the MIB.

Roger Snook

The technical director of the MIB. Roger knows the Agreements inside out and lectures extensively on them.

Trevor Harrison

The operations manager. He has good knowledge of the Agreements and should be a good starting point for contacting the MIB when you have a problem that cannot be resolved with the person conducting the claim.

1.6.2   The MIB contact details

Registered Office address

Motor Insurers' Bureau
Linford Wood House
6–12 Capital Drive
Milton Keynes
MK14 6XT

Telephone number

01908 830001

Fax number

01908 671681

Document exchange address

142620 Milton Keynes 10[23]

---

23   Remember that the service of notices on the MIB is not permitted by document exchange. See 2.3.2.1.

1.7   FORMS

F1   Instructions to the enquiry agent to locate the insurer/identify the driver

CLAIMANT DETAILS			
Reference number			
Name			
Address			
Telephone numbers	H(ome)	W(ork)	M(obile)
ACCIDENT DETAILS			
Date of accident			
Location			
THIRD PARTY DRIVER DETAILS			
Name			
Address			
Telephone numbers	H	W	M
Description – height/weight/sex/ hair colour			
VEHICLE OWNER/KEEPER'S DETAILS (IF DIFFERENT FROM DRIVER)			
Name			
Address			
Telephone numbers	H	W	M
Description – height/weight/sex/ hair colour			
POLICE INVOLVEMENT			
Station address			
Station telephone number			
Officer attending (name/number)			

Please visit the driver and/or the registered keeper of the vehicle and attempt to obtain insurance details. Subsequently, it may prove necessary to use your evidence to confirm the identity of the driver at the time of the accident. Therefore, please take detailed notes of your attendance upon the driver, particularly concentrating on the identity of the driver (a detailed description of the driver's appearance) and any evidence which confirms he was the driver of the vehicle at the time of the accident. Please provide a witness statement incorporating all relevant details for the purpose of confirming the identity of the driver.

CHAPTER 2

THE 1999 UNINSURED DRIVERS AGREEMENT

CHAPTER SUMMARY

2.1	**Introduction**	☐
2.2	**The basic Agreement**	☐
2.3	**Conditions precedent**	☐
2.3.1	The application form (Clause 7)	☐
2.3.2	The notice requirements	☐
2.3.2.1	Method of service of notices (Clause 8)	☐
2.3.2.2	Notice of issue of proceedings (Clause 9)	☐
2.3.2.3	Notice of service of proceedings (Clause 10)	☐
2.3.2.4	Other notices (Clause 11)	☐
2.3.3	Section 154 of the Road Traffic Act 1988 (Clause 13)	☐
2.4	**Exceptions and limitations**	☐
2.4.1	Children and persons not of full capacity (Clause 3)	☐
2.4.2	Exclusions by knowledge: 'the passenger exceptions'	☐
2.4.2.1	Knowledge that the driver was uninsured	☐
2.4.2.2	The burden and standard of proof of such knowledge	☐
2.4.2.3	Knowledge that the vehicle was stolen	☐
2.4.2.4	Knowledge that the vehicle was being used in the course of or furtherance of a crime	☐
2.4.3	Excluded vehicles	☐
2.4.4	The use of vehicles not required to be covered by contracts of insurance (Clause 6(1)(b))	☐
2.4.5	Limitations; property damage	☐
2.5	**The Revised Notes for Guidance 2002**	☐
2.6	**The MIB reserving their position on notices**	☐
2.7	**Checklist**	☐
CL1	Excluded vehicles list	☐
2.8	**Standard letters**	☐
L1	Letter to the MIB regarding reserved notice point	☐

2.1 INTRODUCTION

In studying the 1999 Agreement, we have not had the advantage of many cases being tested, as the Agreement is still relatively new. More pertinent is the fact that the 1999 Agreement has only just been in force for three years. Past knowledge of the MIB's conduct of cases shows that the MIB will not take cases challenging notices given until the three year limitation period has passed, so that if the MIB is successful, it knows that the claimant cannot simply reissue proceedings.

Proceed on the basis that where the MIB can take points, it will do so. The only way to ensure that the MIB is not allowed to take any opportunity of avoiding your claim is to comply exactly with the terms of the Agreement. It is important to remember that the MIB's liability to satisfy the judgment obtained against an uninsured driver is effectively a contractual one arising out of the 1999 Agreement; therefore, if the terms are not complied with, a court cannot exercise any discretion to waive the breach, however unfair the result will otherwise be.[1] Such breaches are likely to lead to claims being struck out and in turn, professional negligence claims against the solicitors involved being instigated.

The only way that the court could effectively excuse the breach would be if it found that the MIB had waived the breach and/or was estopped from taking that point through its own actions.[2] Therefore, if a breach has occurred after issue of proceedings but prior to the expiry of the limitation period, the MIB should immediately be requested to confirm in writing that it will not rely on such a breach to avoid its liability to satisfy an outstanding judgment at a later date, and in the absence of clear and written confirmation, proceedings should be withdrawn and reissued.[3]

---

1   See for instance *Silverton v Goodall* [1997] PIQR 451, where, in a case under the 1988 Agreement, the claimant's solicitors did not give the MIB the requisite notice of issue within the relevant time period and served it late because the court did not send the notice to the claimant's solicitors until after that time period had expired (due to unexplained delays in the court office). The claimant's solicitors subsequently joined the MIB as a defendant, and that claim was struck out due to their failure to comply with the notice period. The Court of Appeal upheld that decision. Similarly, in *Cambridge v Callaghan* (1997) The Times, 21 March, the Court of Appeal held that the MIB did not have to satisfy a judgment where a copy of an unstamped writ or notice of issue was served.

2   See for instance *Begum v Ullah and MIB* [1998] CLY 590, where the court did not give the claimant's solicitors notice of issue of proceedings until after the deadline for notice to be given to the MIB had expired. The claimant's solicitors telephoned the MIB and an employee agreed to waive the notice requirement. The relevant documentation was sent to the MIB the following day. Only after the expiry of the limitation period did the MIB seek to assert that proper notice had not been given. The circuit judge held that the MIB had waived its right to rely upon the deadline and the claimant had altered her position in reliance thereon as, otherwise she could have withdrawn proceedings and reissued them, ensuring the correct notice was given.

3   See 2.8, letter L1.

2.2   THE BASIC AGREEMENT

The MIB is obliged to satisfy outstanding judgments[4] in cases where legislation requires that the relevant liability be insured against by the user of a vehicle. This obligation only arises where the claimant concerned has complied with various conditions (see 2.3 below) and is limited or absent in certain circumstances (see 2.4 below). In practice, the MIB will not wait for the judgment to be entered before seeking involvement; as with an insurer, it will enter into correspondence and negotiations prior to the issue of proceedings.

2.3   CONDITIONS PRECEDENT

The 1999 Agreement sets out various conditions, breach of which will result in the MIB not being liable to satisfy the judgment.

2.3.1   The application form (Clause 7)

The application form[5] must be fully completed and provided to the MIB or no liability to satisfy any judgment will be incurred. It is advisable to submit it as soon as it has been fully completed and ensure that it is signed by the claimant.[6] It must be lodged no later than 14 days after the commencement of proceedings.[7] See 5.3 below for further information about completion of the application form.

2.3.2   The notice requirements[8]

These represent onerous procedural hurdles that must be precisely dealt with or no liability to satisfy judgment will attach to the MIB. The draconian effects of non-compliance, together with the significant number of deadlines to be met, are likely to lead to a rush of professional negligence claims against solicitors as the three year limitation period for claims under this Agreement begins to expire.

---

4   Clause 5(1) of the 1999 Agreement provides that the MIB's obligation is to satisfy a judgment which is not satisfied in full within seven days of the date of judgment being entered.

5   The application form should be obtained from the MIB – see 1.6.2. Such forms may be updated from time to time, so ensure that any form used has been recently obtained.

6   Clause 7(2) states that the MIB can refuse to accept any application unless it is reasonably satisfied that the claimant is fully aware of the contents of the application and its effect.

7   See the Revised Notes for Guidance 2002, Clause 5(3), and also Clause 5(1), which allow 21 days from the date of proceedings where the claimant is not legally represented.

8   These are dealt with in Chapters 4, 5, 6 and 7 as they become necessary.

2.3.2.1   Method of service of notices (Clause 8)

The 1999 Agreement states that the notices referred to in Clauses 9–12 shall only be sufficiently given or supplied if sent by fax or registered or recorded delivery[9] to the MIB's registered office[10] and delivery shall be proved only by the production of the transmission report or an appropriate postal receipt.[11] Service by fax provides immediate confirmation of sending the document. The fee-earner with conduct of the claim should submit the fax, as he is the person who will be best placed to give evidence in court if the MIB state that the fax was never received. A copy of the fax confirmation sheet should be retained and attached to the letter providing notice of issue to the MIB. Ensure that the correct number of pages have fed through the fax machine.

2.3.2.2   Notice of issue of proceedings (Clause 9)

The 1999 Agreement states that the MIB will incur no liability unless it (or the relevant insurer) receives written notice that proceedings have been issued and a copy of the sealed claim form or writ, together with a number of other documents,[12] within 14 days of the commencement of proceedings.[13] The claimant's solicitors must remember that to omit just one of the required documents will lead to the MIB being able to avoid liability to satisfy the judgment, even if such a document has been served at an earlier stage, unless it was served with the application form under Clause 7.

The particulars of claim (and the documents which have to be served therewith under the Civil Procedure Rules) is one of the documents that must be served within the 'Proper Notice' requirements, save that where it was not served with the claim form, a copy must be served not later than seven days after it is served on the defendant.[14]

2.3.2.3   Notice of service of proceedings (Clause 10)

The MIB will incur no liability under the 1999 Agreement unless the claimant gives it written notice within seven days of either:

---

9   Registered post has now been replaced by Special Delivery. Use only fax or recorded delivery until the Agreement is amended to refer to Special Delivery.

10   See 1.6.2.

11   The Revised Notes for Guidance 2002 concede that: 'If the claimant proves that service by DX, First Class Post, Personal Service or any other form of service allowed by the Civil Procedure Rules was effected, the MIB will accept that such notice has been served in the same circumstances in which a party to litigation would be obliged to accept that he had been validly served by such means.' Oddly, however, this concession does not appear to be extended to other notices required to be served upon the MIB. For the avoidance of doubt, all notices should be served by fax or recorded delivery: see footnote 9 above.

12   See 5.4 below.

13   See footnotes to 2.1 for examples of cases where notice periods were missed under the 1988 Agreement.

14   Clause 9(3).

(a) notice from the court that service of the claim form has occurred; or

(b) notice from the defendant that service has occurred; or

(c) the date of personal service; or

(d) within 14 days of the deemed date of service,

whichever of those dates occurs first.

Therefore, the claimant cannot rely on the court notification as, if he is notified after the 14 day period from when the defendant was actually served, it will already be too late. The court should never be allowed to issue and serve proceedings where the MIB is involved.

2.3.2.4   Other notices (Clause 11)

Clause 11 sets out a number of further notices which need to be given no later than seven days after the occurrence of the event in question (NOT seven days after the claimant has been given notice of the occurrence of the event). Failure to supply these notices will again lead to the MIB being able to refuse to satisfy an outstanding judgment. These events are:

(a) the filing of a defence (Clause 11(1)(a));

(b) amendments to the particulars of claim, schedule or other documents required to be served therewith (Clause 11(1)(b));

  (In both cases, copies of the relevant documents need to be served along with the notice.)

(c) setting down of the case for trial by the claimant (Clause 11(1)(c)(i));

(d) where the court gives notice to the claimant of the trial date, the date when that notice was received (Clause 11(1)(c)(ii)).

Further, the MIB will incur no liability unless the claimant provides 'within a reasonable time' any additional information and documents that the MIB reasonably requires.[15]

2.3.3   Section 154 of the Road Traffic Act 1988 (Clause 13)

The MIB can refuse to satisfy the judgment if the claimant fails, as soon as is reasonably practicable, to demand the insurance details from the other driver

---

15 See *Dray v Doherty* (1999) Current Law Cases, Ref 99/525, in which the MIB requested copies of the affidavit of service and copies relating to orders regarding service (amongst other things) within seven days. The claimant's solicitors served the same after 20 days, at which point the MIB applied for a declaration that it did not have to satisfy the judgment due to the failure to comply with the equivalent clause in the 1988 Agreement. The court held that the MIB was still liable to satisfy the judgment, holding that the seven day deadline was not necessary, appropriate or reasonable. However, the Agreement states that the Secretary of State should determine what is reasonable as regards the MIB (Clause 19).

and, in the event of the driver failing to comply, to make a formal complaint to the police, and to use all reasonable endeavours to obtain the name and address of the registered keeper.[16]

The Revised Notes for Guidance 2002 suggest that such obligations will be met if the MIB application form has been sufficiently completed and signed by the claimant; however, this should not be relied upon.

2.4   EXCEPTIONS AND LIMITATIONS

2.4.1   Children and persons not of full capacity (Clause 3)

This clause states that where any act is done to or by a solicitor or other person acting on behalf of the claimant, any decision is made by or in respect of a solicitor or any other person acting on behalf of a claimant, or any sum is paid to a solicitor or any other person acting on behalf of claimant, then, whatever the age or circumstances of the claimant, that act shall be treated as if done to a claimant of full age and capacity.

This attempts to remove most of the protection currently afforded to claimants who are persons not of full capacity or children, for no reason which could be regarded as in their or the public's interest. On any reasonable interpretation, it suggests that, certainly once an adult consults a solicitor or makes an application to the MIB, the three year limitation period would start to run.

The Revised Notes for Guidance 2002 state that 'nothing in the Agreement is intended to vary the limitation rules applying to claimants not of full age or capacity. Limitation for personal injury remains three years from the date of full age or capacity'. Where proceedings have been issued outside the three year time limit, it would be possible to argue that these Notes for Guidance effectively constitute a waiver by the MIB and thus prevent it from relying on Clause 3. Therefore, it will always be safer to issue within three years of the accident, even when the claimant is below 18 or not of full capacity. See 2.5 below.

If the clause is not intended to change the limitation period, it is difficult to see what it is intended to cover. It seems to suggest that, for instance, on settlement, it will not be necessary to issue Part 8 proceedings for court approval of the settlement, as such sums paid by the MIB to the solicitor will be treated as though paid to a claimant of full age or capacity. However, this is in direct conflict with the Civil Procedure Rules and a claimant solicitor should insist that the usual procedures are followed.

---

16   See Chapter 4 for practical tips to deal with this.

2.4.2 Exclusions by knowledge: 'the passenger exceptions'

The 1999 Agreement prevents recovery from the MIB by claimants if they knew that the driver was uninsured.[17] This arises only with passengers within the vehicle driven by the uninsured driver. There are further bars to the recovery of claimants who were passengers within the uninsured driver's car if they knew that the vehicle was stolen or that the vehicle was being used for some form of criminal enterprise.

2.4.2.1 Knowledge that the driver was uninsured

The 1999 Agreement allows the MIB to avoid satisfying a judgment where the claimant knew or ought to have known that there was no policy of insurance in force for the vehicle in which he was travelling. The term 'knew or ought to have known' must be interpreted restrictively[18] and if an ordinary prudent passenger, with the same facts and knowledge available to him as were available to the claimant, would have made enquiries as to the existence of insurance for the vehicle, the claimant's carelessness or negligence is not sufficient to allow the MIB to avoid the claim under this permitted exception.

2.4.2.2 The burden and standard of proof of such knowledge

Under the 1988 Agreement (and the 1972 Agreement), the MIB had to prove on the balance of probabilities that the passenger knew or ought to have known that the driver was uninsured.[19]

Under the 1999 Agreement however, there is a shift of the burden of proof in certain cases, and claimant solicitors should be wary of this.

Clause 6(3) states that whilst the burden of proving that the claimant knew or ought to have known that the defendant was uninsured is on the MIB, the proof of any one of the following matters shall be taken as proof of the

---

17 Clause 6(1)(d).

18 *White v White and Another* [2001] UKHL 9; [2001] 1 WLR 481; [2001] 2 All ER 43; [2001] PIQR 20. The House of Lords held that unless the claimant had actual knowledge that the driver was not insured or had information from which he had drawn the conclusion that the driver might not be insured but had deliberately refrained from asking, lest his suspicions should be confirmed, then the claimant had not 'known or ought to have known'.

19 See *Porter v MIB* [1978] RTR 503, where the claimant owned a vehicle which she requested the defendant to drive. The defendant was uninsured. It was held that as she had no reason to suspect that he was uninsured, and that she had seen him driving at work, the MIB had failed to prove that she knew or ought to have known and had to satisfy the judgment.

claimant's knowledge that he was uninsured, unless there is evidence to the contrary. Those matters are:

(1) that the claimant was the owner or registered keeper of the vehicle or had caused or permitted its use;

(2) that the claimant knew the vehicle was being used by a person below the minimum age at which he could be granted a licence to drive that vehicle;

(3) that the claimant knew that the person driving the vehicle was disqualified from holding or obtaining a driving licence; and

(4) that the claimant knew that the user of the vehicle was neither its owner nor registered keeper, nor an employee of the owner or registered keeper, nor the owner or registered keeper of any other vehicle.

Even in the case of an under-age or disqualified defendant, the MIB will still have to prove that the claimant knew that he was under-age or disqualified. These extra exceptions merely shift the burden of proof as only 'in the absence of evidence to the contrary' is the requisite knowledge found to be proved; it will not necessarily prove to be fatal to the claim.

2.4.2.3   Knowledge that the vehicle was stolen

Under the 1999 Agreement, no liability will be incurred by the MIB where the passenger 'knew or ought to have known[20] that the vehicle had been stolen or unlawfully taken' when he entered the vehicle or after he got in but when he still had a reasonable opportunity to get out.

2.4.2.4   Knowledge that the vehicle was being used in the course of or furtherance of a crime

Under the 1999 Agreement, two specific exclusions are introduced where the passenger knew (or ought to have known) that the vehicle was being used in the course of or furtherance of a crime, or that it was being used as a means of escape from, or avoidance of, lawful apprehension.

Drunk drivers

In normal personal injury cases, where the claimant was a passenger who knew that the driver was over the legal limit, a deduction for contributory negligence would be applied. However, as driving with excess alcohol is a criminal offence, knowledge that the driver was driving under the influence would result in knowledge that the vehicle was being used in the course of or furtherance of a crime, and therefore the passenger claiming under the 1999 Agreement would be unable to recover any damages from the MIB.

---

20   See footnote 18 and the case of *White v White and Another* [2001] UKHL 9; [2001] 1 WLR 481; [2001] 2 All ER 43; [2001] PIQR 20.

Knowledge that the passenger had or ought to have had for the purposes of any of these exceptions includes knowledge that the passenger could have reasonably been expected to have had, had he not been under the self-induced influence of drink or drugs. Therefore, the defence that, although it may have been evident to others that the driver was drunk, the passenger's own intoxication prevented it from being evident to him does not assist.[21]

Drugs

Driving under the influence of drugs is illegal and therefore the passenger who has entered into the vehicle of a driver who he knows to be under such influence will be similarly excluded from claiming damages. It is less clear-cut where the passenger knows that there are illegal substances within the vehicle but not that the driver is driving under their influence. If the presence of the substances is merely incidental to the journey (the driver and passenger's personal supply of heroin being within the car, for instance), then the passenger should still be able to claim, as the vehicle is not being used either in the course of the crime or for the furtherance of it. If the journey was to deliver or collect drugs, then the passenger could be excluded from claiming. This matter has yet to be tested in the courts, however.

Dangerous driving/driving without due care and attention

Almost all of these cases will involve a standard of driving by the driver that will involve the commission of the offence of either dangerous driving or driving without due care and attention; the issue will be whether the passenger knew that the standard of driving was likely to be such when he entered the vehicle or whether, after it became evident that it was, he had an opportunity to remove himself from the vehicle. A prolonged course of dangerous driving, during which the passenger had the opportunity to leave the vehicle, may lead to the MIB being able to refuse to satisfy any judgment.

Other criminal activity

Where the MIB satisfies the court that the claimant knew of other criminal activity, the issue will be whether the vehicle was being used in the course or furtherance of the crime, or was merely incidental to it.[22] The passenger of a

---

21 Clause 6(4).

22 There is as yet no case law on the interpretation of this point. Some assistance may be gained from the case law resulting from s 143 of the Powers of Criminal Courts (Sentencing) Act 2000, which enables courts to deprive offenders of property 'used for the purpose of committing, or facilitating the commission of any offence'. Orders have been upheld in relation to vehicles used for transporting stolen property (R v Lidster [1976] RTR 240), whilst an order was quashed in relation to a vehicle in which a girl was indecently assaulted, as the offender did not intend to commit the offence when the girl entered the car (R v Lucas (1975) unreported, 4 July).

getaway driver for a bank robbery will not be able to claim. This exception is likely to be construed against the passenger; there will be little sympathy for the passenger who knew that the driver was engaged in any criminal conduct and decided to accept a lift.

2.4.3 Excluded vehicles

The MIB excludes claims where the vehicle is a Crown vehicle unless the vehicle is insured. If there is no insurance in place then the Crown or the relevant authority deals with the claim directly. Other vehicles are also excluded from claims against the MIB and are summarised in the checklist at 2.7.

2.4.4 The use of vehicles not required to be covered by contracts of insurance (Clause 6(1)(b))

This clause exempts the MIB from having to satisfy judgments when the claim arises out of the use of a vehicle which is not required to be covered by insurance – the 'off-road' exception. Prior to 3 April 2000, vehicles only required insurance when they were being used on a public road and therefore accidents off public roads would not lead to any liability on the MIB to satisfy the judgment.[23] Since that date, however, legislation[24] has widened the scope of compulsory insurance to include the use of vehicles on any 'road or other public place' and therefore a claimant will be able to recover from the MIB when the accident occurred off-road but in a public place.[25]

2.4.5 Limitations; property damage

See 8.1.1, below.

2.5 THE REVISED NOTES FOR GUIDANCE 2002[26]

The Notes for Guidance, published with the Agreement and subsequently revised are intended by the MIB to offer assistance to those interpreting the Agreement. However, it must be noted that the preamble of the Notes states:

---

23 See for instance *Clarke v Kato* [1998] 1 WLR 1647; [1998] 4 All ER 417; [1998] PIQR 1, in which the House of Lords held that the MIB did not have to satisfy two judgments obtained against uninsured drivers who had negligently injured innocent third parties in a multi-storey car park and on the kerb of a car park, neither place being defined as a 'road'.

24 Motor Vehicles (Compulsory Insurance) Regulations 2000.

25 The definition of 'public place' will be one of fact; for instance, a pub car park at closing time is undoubtedly a public place, but at 3 am when there is no evidence of any realistic prospect of members of the public being present, it may not be. A multi-storey car park would be a public place during its opening hours.

26 See Appendix B.

> The following notes are for the guidance of anyone who may have a claim on the Motor Insurers' Bureau under this Agreement and their legal advisers. They are not part of the Agreement, their purpose being to deal in ordinary language with the situations which most readily occur. They are not in any way a substitute for reading and applying the terms of this or any other relevant Agreement.

This seems to suggest that the court can only look to them for assistance at times when there is some doubt as to the Agreement's meaning.

The Revised Notes (in which many concessions are made) state that:

> [A]t the request of the Secretary of State, these notes have been revised with effect from[27] ... and in their revised form have been agreed and approved by the MIB, the Law Society of England and Wales, the Law Society of Scotland, the Motor Accident Solicitors Society and the Association of Personal Injury Lawyers. Any application made under the Agreement after this date (unless proceedings have already been issued) will be handled by MIB in accordance with these notes.

These concessions do not form part of the Agreement itself therefore and solicitors should be wary of relying on such concessions unless absolutely necessary. It is best to comply with the strict terms of the Agreement and only in the event of an unfortunate breach should you rely on the Notes to argue that the MIB is estopped from raising the particular point (or has waived its right to rely on such a clause).

The Revised Notes are set out in full in Appendix B. The MIB has confirmed in writing to the Motor Accident Solicitors Society, the Law Society and the Association of Personal Injury Lawyers that they will apply the Revised Notes for Guidance to all cases under the 1999 Uninsured Drivers Agreement from 15 April 2002, where proceedings were not already issued, irrespective of the accident date.

2.6   THE MIB RESERVING THEIR POSITION ON NOTICES

Letter L1

Under the 1988 Uninsured Drivers Agreement, if proceedings were issued and notice was purported to be given to the MIB in accordance with the Agreement, but that notice was invalid, the MIB would sometimes draw the invalid notice to the attention of the claimant's solicitor, and would reserve the right to take

---

27   15 April 2002 was the agreed date for finalisation of the Notes, but the MIB confirm they will apply them to all cases proceeding under the 1999 Agreement, where proceedings had not been issued before that date.

the point in respect of that notice at a later date. The MIB could then wait for the limitation period to expire, and then take the notice point, knowing that proceedings could not then be reissued.

All files should be checked to ensure that this has not occurred on files proceeding under the 1999 Uninsured Drivers Agreement. If the MIB has reserved its position in relation to a notice point, it should be asked to confirm in writing that it will at no time in the future take the notice point. The letter should also refer to the costs of the discontinued proceedings. Unless the MIB provides unequivocal confirmation that it will not take the notice point reserved at a later date, new proceedings should be issued before the limitation period has expired.[28]

2.7   CHECKLIST

CL1   Excluded vehicles list

Crown vehicles

Is the vehicle owned by or in the possession of the Crown?

If yes, is the vehicle insured (insurance company deals)?

If no, did someone take over the responsibility for the existence of contract of insurance (if yes, direct the claim to that person)?

If no, the Crown to deal with the claim.

Vehicles not required to be covered by contract of insurance (although may be so covered)

Does the vehicle fit within one of the following categories?

(i)   The vehicle is owned by a person who has deposited £500,000 for the Accountant General of the Supreme Court and is being driven under the owner's control.

(ii)   Council/local authority vehicle.

(iii) Police authority vehicle.

(iv)   National criminal intelligence/national crime squad vehicles.

(v)   The vehicle is being driven on a journey to or from any place undertaken for salvage purposes pursuant to Part IX of the Merchant Shipping Act 1995.

(vi)   Vehicles being used under the Army Act 1955 or the Airforce Act 1955.

(vii) Vehicles owned by a Health Service body.

---

28   See 2.8, letter L1.

(viii) Ambulances owned by a National Health Service Trust.

(ix) A vehicle made available by the Secretary of State to any person, body or local authority pursuant to s 23 or 26 of the National Health Act 1977.

(x)   A vehicle made available by the Secretary of State to any local authority, education authority or voluntary organisation in Scotland pursuant to s 15 or 16 of the National Health Services (Scotland) Act 1978.

If yes, then this is not an MIB claim. The claim will be settled by an insurer if one exists, or the authority concerned.

2.8 STANDARD LETTERS

L1 Letter to the MIB regarding reserved notice point

Motor Insurers' Bureau
[Registered Office]

BY FAX AND RECORDED DELIVERY:

Dear

Claimant:
Uninsured driver:
Date of accident:

We refer to your letter dated .... in which you stated notice had not been given in accordance with the 1999 Uninsured Drivers Agreement. However, you confirmed that you would not take the notice point at that time, but reserved your right to do so in the future.

You will appreciate we cannot allow this uncertainty to continue. Unless you provide unequivocal confirmation in writing that at no time in the future will you ask the court or the Secretary of State to determine whether valid notice has been given, we will have no alternative but to discontinue the current proceedings and commence new proceedings providing the correct notice. We will not pay any of your costs of the discontinued proceedings on the basis that the same could be avoided if you provide the written confirmation requested in this letter. We will draw this letter to the attention of the court if required to do so.

Yours

CHAPTER 3

MANAGING MIB CLAIMS WITHIN
A PERSONAL INJURY DEPARTMENT

CHAPTER SUMMARY

3.1   SPECIALIST MIB TEAMS

3.1.1   Need for specialist knowledge

In any reasonably sized firm, there needs to be a specialist MIB team of fee-earners.

There are numerous procedural hurdles, notice requirements and special rules that apply to the 1999 Agreement. Such claims need to be dealt with by those with experience of and speciality in this field, otherwise the fee-earner concerned will spend a large number of unchargeable hours researching the law. The pooling together of such specialist knowledge provides an invaluable resource within the firm.

3.1.2   Need for different approaches and systems

Those dealing with claims against the MIB need to work on them in a different way to normal personal injury claims.[1] The notice requirements necessitate files

---

1   For instance, routine service of documents on the MIB should be done by fax or recorded delivery – see 2.3.2.1 for details.

being reviewed at least every seven days once proceedings have been issued, as many of the provisions in the 1999 Agreement compel notification of the MIB of developments within seven days of them occurring;[2] failure to do so leads to the MIB being able to refuse to settle any subsequent judgment. This also necessitates an intensely proactive approach in chasing other parties, experts and the courts to ensure that deadlines have not been passed prior to the claimant's solicitor receiving the relevant document.[3] Such weekly reviews, proactive chasing and immediate response to communications received need to be continued whilst the fee-earner is on holiday or absent through sickness – hence the need for a dedicated team, alive to the particular issues and urgency that arises in these cases.

Being proactive with MIB cases will also increase the opportunity of settling the claims within the three year limitation period, thereby avoiding the need to issue proceedings and comply with the numerous post-issue requirements.

A standard practice, within the group, of serving every document on the MIB within seven days of receipt will increase the speed at which the claim progresses, and will also make compliance with the seven day notices after issue more straightforward. Serving every document or letter on the MIB by fax as a matter of routine will also help achieve this aim.

3.1.3   Dealing with the MIB

A dedicated team will build up a better working relationship with those within the MIB, hence allowing an early approach to consensual progress and settlement, and also allowing the fee-earners to become accustomed to the MIB's operating procedures. It may be possible to set up discussion facilities with the MIB to negotiate in relation to a number of files at any one time, ensuring that the exercise is a useful and cost-effective one; the MIB is as keen as others within the insurance industry to settle claims at an early stage if possible, not least to save costs.

If there are insufficient files within one firm to warrant a meeting, agree a date with the MIB and ask other firms in your town or city to attend with their own MIB files. Discussion facilities will assist greatly in the attempt to conclude all MIB claims within the three year period, thereby avoiding the need to issue proceedings. See 5.5 for a standard form for discussion meetings.

---

2   See 2.3.2 for details.

3   See for instance *Silverton v Goodall* [1997] PIQR 451, where, in a case under the 1988 Agreement, the claimant's solicitors did not give the MIB the requisite notice of issue within the relevant time period and served it late because the court did not send the notice to the claimant's solicitors until after that time period had expired (due to unexplained delays in the court office). The claimant's solicitors subsequently joined the MIB as a defendant, and that claim was struck out due to their failure to comply with the notice period. The Court of Appeal upheld that decision.

3.1.4   Restriction of caseloads for fee-earners

Being able to allocate work within the specialist team should ensure that an individual fee-earner does not become overburdened with too many active MIB cases; a caseload of 100 such cases on which proceedings have been issued will necessitate the review of 20 files each day, dealing with correspondence and telephone calls, and still needs to allow a proactive approach to be maintained.

3.1.5   MIB communications

The MIB team should adopt a specific MIB reference (so that the person receiving incoming communications recognises the need for urgency). There should also be a specific procedure whereby, if any communication (letter or document) is received on an MIB file, it is immediately forwarded to an individual within the MIB team, preventing such communications from lying on a desk overlooked for a few days, by which time deadlines may have been missed. In view of the importance of the seven day deadlines, communications on MIB cases need to be treated as if received through recorded delivery and the receipt signed for.[4] This will avoid the post being left unattended and a seven day notice being missed. It also allows the fee-earner with conduct of the case the maximum opportunity of complying with any seven day notice relating to the communication.

3.1.6   Case management

The MIB team can prepare precedent letters, documents and case management systems (examples are given throughout this book) to ensure that the correct format of notice is used with the correct enclosures. The case management system will have to be specifically adapted from the usual personal injury one adopted by the firm to ensure such claims are expedited and settled if at all possible prior to limitation, and to ensure that there is an automatic diary entry for review of the file at least once every seven days after the issue of proceedings. This should appear in more than one person's diary system to cover sickness and holidays.

3.1.6.1   Issuing proceedings

In all MIB cases, proceedings should be issued well before the expiry of the limitation period, and sensibly no later than two and a half years after the incident date. This has three benefits:

(1) it removes the uncertainty relating to claimants not of full capacity;[5]

---

4   See 3.2, document D1.
5   See 2.4.1.

(2) if notice periods are not complied with, proceedings can be reissued within the three year limitation period and the correct notices given;

(3) any difficulties which arise in serving the driver can be resolved prior to the expiry of the limitation period.[6]

3.1.7   The MIB claims register

> Document D2

The MIB team should have a centralised MIB claims register to keep account of how many active MIB cases there are within the firm.

---

6   See 5.2.

D1

MIB COMMUNICATION

RECEIPT FORM

One of these forms must be completed for each item of MIB post received.

The post and this form must be delivered to the fee-earner within 30 minutes of receipt and a signature for the document must be obtained.

If the fee-earner is not available, obtain a receipt from another member of the team, or other support staff within the same team.

Once signed for, copy the form and leave the copy with the fee-earner.

The original must be returned to the post room.

CASE REF	DOCUMENT	TIME/DATE OF RECEIPT	DELIVERED BY/TO? (Print name)	SIGN RECEIPT (Both)	TIME OF RECEIPT	MIB NOTICE REQUIRED? (Specify)	NOTICE GIVEN?

D2

MIB CLAIMS REGISTER

File ref	Date of knowledge	Fee-earner	Which Agreement? 1999 UIDA 1988 UIDA UNTRACED	No of claimants	Demand for TPD insurance made? Y/N?	Police complaint made?	Any other comments

CHAPTER 4

RECEIPT OF INSTRUCTIONS

The 1999 Agreement imposes strict time limits not only on the solicitor but also on the client, and there is, therefore, potential that the client will be already dangerously close to breaching the Agreement at the time of the first contact with the solicitor. A detailed first interview is therefore necessary, together with a series of actions which will need to be undertaken immediately on receipt of instructions.

CHAPTER SUMMARY

4.1	**Action to be taken**	☐
4.1.1	Establish the driver's identity	☐
4.1.2	Request insurance details from the driver	☐
4.1.3	Endeavour to trace the registered keeper	☐
4.1.4	Request insurance details from the registered keeper and report	☐
4.1.5	Trace the insurer	☐
4.1.6	Complaint to the police	☐
4.1.7	Obtain correspondence between the client and the driver	☐
4.1.8	Obtain insurance policies from the client	☐
4.2	**Issues to consider**	☐
4.2.1	Children and persons not of full capacity	☐
4.2.2	The passenger of the uninsured driver	☐
4.2.2.1	Knowledge that the driver was uninsured	☐
4.2.2.2	Knowledge that the vehicle was stolen	☐
4.2.2.3	Knowledge that the vehicle was being used in the course of or in furtherance of a crime	☐
4.2.3	Other exceptions that may apply	☐
4.2.3.1	Crown vehicles	☐
4.2.3.2	Off-road accidents	☐
4.3	**Standard letters**	☐
L2	First letter to the client dealing with relevant issues	☐
L3	Letter for the client to forward to the driver	☐
L4	Letter to the driver from the solicitor	☐
L5	Letter to the police regarding failure to supply insurance policy details	☐
L6	Letter to be sent with DVLA search form	☐

L7	Letter to the registered keeper from the solicitor	☐
L8	Letter to the police regarding the registered keeper's failure to provide details	☐
4.4	**Client questionnaire**	☐
Q1	MIB Questionnaire	☐
4.5	**Diary entries**	☐

4.1   ACTION TO BE TAKEN

4.1.1   Establish the driver's identity

Letter L2

Obtain a full and detailed description of the driver, together with the originals or copies of any documents that he produced, and pieces of paper on which he wrote down any details, during the first interview and put all the information into a statement to be signed by your client. If there is any doubt about the identity of a driver, the MIB will attempt to have the claim dealt with under the terms of the Untraced Drivers Agreement, thereby avoiding the need for them to pay your reasonable costs. Thus, it is essential to have as much information as possible at the beginning of the claim, in order that you can prove, on the balance of probabilities, that you have identified the driver and the claim should be dealt with as an uninsured and not an untraced one.[1]

If there is any doubt about the identity of the driver, an Untraced Drivers Agreement application form must be lodged with the MIB within three years of the date of the accident,[2] regardless of the capacity of the claimant. As it is not known at the beginning of the claim whether it will become an untraced claim, a paragraph demanding that the claimant report the matter to the police within 14 days of the accident should be included in the first letter to the client.[3]

---

1   This is particularly relevant if there are suspicions that the driver has given a false name; proceedings issued against a non-existent person will not succeed and therefore the MIB will not have to satisfy the judgment. A similar scenario will arise if it is later discovered that the driver has given the details of an innocent party. If judgment is not obtained against the person against whom proceedings were issued, then there is no judgment for the MIB to satisfy, and by that stage it may be too late to proceed under the Untraced Drivers Agreement. See 13.3 for conditions precedent to the Untraced Drivers Agreement.

2   Clause 1(1)(f) of the Untraced Drivers Agreement 1996.

3   Clause 1(1)(g) of the Untraced Drivers Agreement 1996; see 4.3, letter L2.

4.1.2   Request insurance details from the driver

Letters L3 and L4

An immediate demand for insurance details from the driver must be made. The 1999 Agreement states that the demand must be made as soon as reasonably practicable by the claimant.[4] For the avoidance of doubt, the solicitor must also do this immediately and, unless the client has a copy of a letter requesting such details, a letter from both solicitor and client must be dispatched immediately upon receipt of instructions, stating that such demand is made pursuant to s 154 of the Road Traffic Act 1988.[5]

In the interests of saving time and money, it is also worthwhile telephoning the driver if a number is available or can be discovered (and keeping a full attendance note) both within and outside office hours. Even after three years of negotiating with the MIB, proceedings will still have to be issued against and served on the driver; it is therefore important that you trace and retain the driver's contact details.[6] This action may also lead to the location of an insurer, so can be time well spent.

4.1.3   Endeavour to trace the registered keeper

Letters L3, L4 and L6

As outlined in 1.2.2, if there was insurance for the vehicle, albeit not for that particular driver, then the insurance company involved may have to satisfy the judgment. It is therefore important that the registered keeper is traced, in order to discover whether that person has insurance for the vehicle.

Attempting to locate the keeper of the vehicle must at least include the following:

(i)   DVLA search.[7]

(ii) Writing to the driver of the vehicle.[8]

---

4   Clause 13(a) – note that this is by the claimant not by the claimant's solicitor, so the 'as soon as reasonably practicable' period starts to run from the time of the accident and in normal circumstances would mean that the claimant should demand such details at the scene.

5   See 4.3, letters L3 and L4.

6   See 5.2.

7   See 4.3, letter L6.

8   See 4.3, last paragraph in letters L3 and L4.

As it is in your client's interests to find any insurer, sometimes it is worth using an enquiry agent to locate the driver or registered keeper and discover if there is insurance for the vehicle in question. Often an explanation that the insurer can void the driver's policy if he does not report an accident is sufficient to persuade such a person to provide the necessary details.

4.1.4 Request insurance details from the registered keeper and report

Letters L3 and L4

If you discover the name and address of the registered keeper of the vehicle, also demand the insurance details from them. If they have insurance and you have identified the driver of the vehicle, the insurers will have to deal with the claim as RTA insurers even if the vehicle was stolen.[9] If no response is received from the registered keeper, a complaint should be made to the police (see 4.1.6 below).

4.1.5 Trace the insurer

It is vital that investigations to trace any insurer should be put in hand immediately; much of the work that needs to be done in pursuing a claim against the MIB will be obviated if there is an insurer (and if carried out and then found to be unnecessary, it is unlikely that such costs will be allowed on assessment at a later stage).

Investigations should include the following:

- The Motor Insurance Database.
- DVLA searches.
- Telephone enquiries.
- Internet enquiries.
- Personal enquiries.

For full details, see 1.2.1–1.2.1.5.

---

9   See 1.2.2.

4.1.6   Complaint to the police

```
Letter L5
```

If the driver does not supply insurance details, the claimant must make a formal complaint to the police as soon as reasonably practical[10] (Clause 13(b)(i)). A copy of the letter and proof of sending it should be kept as the requirement of this clause is a prerequisite to receiving compensation.[11] Most police forces will take no action, but the complaint must be made to comply with the strict requirements of the Agreement.

If you receive instructions from accident management companies or legal expense insurance companies, which carry out initial enquiries and correspondence, ensure that they are aware of these requirements and make the demands on the claimant's behalf upon receipt of instructions.

4.1.7   Obtain correspondence between the client and the driver

Correspondence between the client (and anyone acting on his behalf)[12] and the driver (and anyone acting on his behalf)[13] must be served with notice of the issue of proceedings to amount to 'Proper Notice',[14] and should be obtained immediately to ensure it is not missed at a later date, which may allow the MIB to avoid paying compensation. The client must be warned that the duty continues, as with all disclosure, and therefore if correspondence is subsequently received, he must forward it to you (see 4.3, letter L2).

4.1.8   Obtain insurance policies from the client

During the first full interview with the client, it is wise to ask him to send you all insurance documents that may be of benefit to him, even if the other driver has insurance. For non-MIB reasons, you will need to see the policies that may

---

10 See 4.3, letter L5.

11 The Revised Notes for Guidance 2002 state that this section does not need to be complied with if the claimant sufficiently completes the application form. However, it is still wise to comply, so that there can be no argument at any later stage.

12 Anyone acting on the claimant's behalf would include legal expense insurers, motor insurers, previous solicitors, current solicitors or any accident management companies – therefore, if the client has previously consulted anyone else about his claim, it is important to ensure that you obtain all copies of correspondence between them and the defendant.

13 Anyone acting on the defendant's behalf would include any potential insurer (even if denying any cover), any legal expense insurer, any solicitor, the registered keeper or any accident management company.

14 See 5.4 and 5.7.

provide your client with benefits when he is in need of them (such as personal accident cover). Also, when proceedings are issued, the MIB has the right to copies or details of any insurance policies providing benefits in the case of death, bodily injury or damage to property to which the proceedings relate where the claimant is the insured party and the benefits are available to him. It is sensible to start to gather this information as soon as possible.[15]

In any event, as your client's legal advisor, you will be anxious to check these to ensure that he claims under any such policies within the requisite time limits, in case the claim against the driver is unsuccessful for some reason or the MIB is held not to be liable to satisfy it.

Which policies should you ask your client to look for and produce? In negotiations in relation to the Revised Notes for Guidance 2002, the MIB suggested that the following are all relevant insurance policies to be provided as 'Proper Notice' when giving notice of issue of proceedings, although this issue has not yet been tested in court:[16]

(1) Vehicle insurance policy.

(2) Private healthcare insurance.

(3) Household insurance.

(4) Credit card policies.

(5) Legal expense insurance policies (although these are probably within (1) and (3) above).[17]

(6) Employers' insurance.[18]

(7) Union benefits policy.

(8) Personal accident cover.

All these items should be listed in the initial standard letter to the client.[19]

4.2 ISSUES TO CONSIDER

There are further issues that have to be considered within the first interview, although in the majority of cases, they will not apply.

---

15 Under Clause 17, the MIB can deduct from the claim any compensation received by the claimant from an insurer or any other source, whilst under Clause 15(b), it can require the claimant to repay any such sum subsequently received, even after judgment. The effect of these clauses on the quantum of the claim is discussed at 8.1.

16 See 9.2.2.

17 These need to be checked to establish the preferred matter of funding the claim in any event.

18 Clause 9(2)(c) specifically limits such policies to those 'where the claimant is the insured party and the benefits are available to him' so it is difficult to believe that his employers' insurance policy will fall into this category, the employers being far more likely to be the insured party; however, if such can be obtained, it should be.

19 See 4.3, letter L2.

4.2.1 Children and persons not of full capacity

Clause 3 of the 1999 Agreement (see 2.4.1) suggests that in some circumstances a child or patient will be treated the same for the purposes of this Agreement as if they were acting with full capacity. It is therefore necessary to ensure the issue of proceedings occurs within the usual three year limitation period rather than relying on the provisions which allow issue within three years of an 18th birthday or of achieving full capacity if under a disability.

4.2.2 The passenger of the uninsured driver

If the client was a passenger within the vehicle of the uninsured driver's car, various exceptions need to be carefully considered, as he may not be entitled to any damages. See 2.4.2 for a full outline of the law in this area. The client questionnaire at 4.4 (Q1) should be completed to enable a full statement to be drafted, dealing with the relevant points at a very early stage; this is likely to be one of the first issues that the MIB will wish to deal with and thus will potentially hold up both negotiations and proceedings.

4.2.2.1 *Knowledge that the driver was uninsured*

See 2.4.2.1. Knowledge that the driver was uninsured will enable the MIB to refuse to satisfy any judgment. The MIB will not necessarily accept your client's contention that he was unaware of the driver's lack of insurance, in which case, it will be a question of fact for the court to decide. The evidence of the uninsured driver (who will usually be the defendant) will be crucial in this respect if he decides to co-operate either with the claimant or the MIB and it is essential that a statement is taken from him if at all possible at a very early stage, dealing solely with this point. The MIB will take a statement from the defendant as well. Other than the defendant and the claimant's evidence on this point, the issues are likely to centre around the length and closeness of the relationship between the claimant and the defendant and therefore whether it was likely that the claimant was aware of the uninsured status of the defendant. Solicitors should be aware of the shift in the burden of proof onto their client in certain cases, which are outlined at 2.4.2.2.

4.2.2.2 *Knowledge that the vehicle was stolen*

See 2.4.2.3 if your client was injured whilst in a stolen vehicle. No liability is incurred by the MIB where the passenger knew or ought to have known that the vehicle had been stolen or unlawfully taken when he entered the vehicle or after he got in but when he still had a reasonable opportunity to get out.

In these cases, it will be important to establish from your client whether there was damage caused to the vehicle in the theft, which will allow the MIB to argue that the passenger must have known that the vehicle was stolen. The crime report should be obtained if possible. If your client has been convicted of being carried in a vehicle taken without the owner's consent as a result of the incident, then the claim can go no further, as such a conviction requires knowledge that the vehicle was stolen or unlawfully taken. Evidence that your client was aware of the defendant having previously stolen vehicles will also have a devastating impact.

4.2.2.3 *Knowledge that the vehicle was being used in the course of or in furtherance of a crime*

See 2.4.2.4. Such crimes include drink driving,[20] driving whilst under the influence of drugs,[21] supplying or delivering drugs, dangerous driving and driving without due care and attention,[22] as well as any other criminal activity.[23] Thus, if the passenger knew that the driver was driving whilst over the legal limit for alcohol, he will be unable to recover any damages at all. Knowledge that your client had or ought to have had for the purposes of any of these exceptions includes knowledge that the passenger could have reasonably been expected to have had, had he not been under the self-induced influence of drink or drugs. Therefore, the defence that, whilst it may have been evident to others that the driver was drunk, etc, the passenger's own intoxication prevented it from being evident to him does not assist.[24]

4.2.3 Other exceptions that may apply

4.2.3.1 *Crown vehicles*

The MIB excludes claims where the vehicle is a Crown vehicle unless the vehicle is insured.[25]

4.2.3.2 *Off-road accidents*

See 2.4.4. The MIB is exempt from satisfying judgments when the claim arises out of the use of a vehicle which is not required to be covered by insurance – the 'off-road' exception. On 3 April 2000, the requirement for insurance was widened from 'roads' to 'roads or other public places' and therefore the MIB will have to satisfy judgments in respect of accidents after that date where the accident occurred off a road but within a public place. To establish that the accident occurred in a public place, evidence will have to be obtained –

---

20 See 2.4.2.4.1.
21 See 2.4.2.4.2.
22 See 2.4.2.4.3.
23 See 2.4.2.4.4.
24 Clause 6(4).
25 See 2.4.3.

photographs or video evidence of the scene at a similar time of day showing that the public had access to it and indeed used it would be particularly helpful. Statements from the owners/occupiers of the land (such as car parks) would also be of assistance.

4.3 STANDARD LETTERS

L2 First letter to the client dealing with relevant issues

This should be sent in all circumstances after the first interview.

Dear

Road accident date:
Other driver's name:

General information explaining the role of the MIB
Your claim for compensation for damages may include a claim against an uninsured driver. The Motor Insurers' Bureau (MIB) is a body set up to pay compensation to the victims of uninsured drivers. However, under the terms of the Uninsured Drivers Agreement, the MIB is able to avoid paying you compensation if you fail to comply with certain requirements. If any of the points are unclear, please telephone me. It is essential that you comply with this letter.

Section regarding reporting the matter to the police (in case it becomes an untraced claim)
I confirm that I have asked you to attend the local police station and report the incident immediately. This is essential. If the identity of the other driver is subsequently discovered to be false, the claim would be dealt with by the MIB, which compensates victims of untraced and uninsured drivers.

The MIB can refuse to compensate you if you fail to notify the police within 14 days of the date of the incident. You must notify the police immediately if you have not already done so. Please ensure you obtain an accident reference number, or at the very least the name of the officer you report the incident to, and send this to me.

Section regarding demand for insurance details
One of the requirements when claiming compensation from the MIB is that you must formally demand from the third party driver details of insurance in respect of the vehicle they were driving, and if you fail to do so, your claim may be rejected. This would leave you with little prospect of recovering any compensation from the driver.

I enclose two copies of a letter, one of which you should complete and send to the driver, the other of which you should also complete in identical terms and return to me, stating that you have sent an identical copy to the driver and when and where you posted it. Please send me any written response you receive from the driver, and in the event of other communication, please advise me as to its nature and contents immediately.

You must send the attached letter immediately.

Demand for details of the client's insurance policies for subsequent disclosure
Another requirement to comply with to ensure you receive compensation if your claim is ultimately successful is that you must supply to the MIB copies of all insurance policies which may provide you with some benefit as a result of the accident (regardless of whether you make a claim under the policy or not).

This will include copies of insurance policies, schedules and certificates covering the following areas:

(1) Vehicle insurance policy.

(2) Private healthcare insurance policy (including your employers' policy if this covers you).

(3) Household contents insurance.

(4) Credit card policies.

(5) Legal expense insurance policies.

(6) Any employers' insurance that benefits you.

(7) Union benefits.

(8) Personal accident cover.

Please forward copies of these policies to me immediately so that I may forward them on to the MIB at the appropriate time. If you subsequently discover any further insurance documentation, this must also be forwarded to me.

Correspondence with the other driver
A further requirement to obtain compensation from the MIB is that you must disclose to it copies of all correspondence between yourself and the following parties:

(a) the driver of the other vehicle; and

(b) his solicitors; and

(c) his insurers; and

(d) his agents (anyone corresponding on his behalf such as family, friends, etc).

Please forward the originals of any correspondence to me immediately. If you do not have any such correspondence, please confirm this in writing. If you have misplaced this correspondence, please confirm the details of the correspondence, including the parties involved, the date and the content of it. If you receive any further correspondence from the defendant or anyone representing him in the future, this must also be forwarded to me.

Please also forward to me copies of the notes you made when you exchanged details with the third party driver at the scene of the accident/shortly afterwards.

Failure to comply fully or at all with any of the above points may result in the MIB avoiding your claim for compensation completely.

I look forward to receiving this information from you as soon as possible.

Yours

L3 Letter for the client to forward to the driver

This must be sent in all circumstances, other than if the client has already sent and provided a copy of such a letter.

Dear

Road accident date:
Location:

You were involved in a road traffic accident with me on the above date.

I formally demand that you supply to me by return post confirmation that you were insured at the time of the accident, or confirmation that you would have been insured if your insurer had not avoided or cancelled your policy.

Please supply full details of your insurance policy including the following:

(a) The vehicle registration numbers covered by the policy of insurance.

(b) The policy number.

(c) The name of the insurer.

(d) The address of the insurer.

(e) The period of the insurance cover.

Please also supply a copy of the insurance policy.

If you were not insured at the time of the accident, please confirm this in writing to me.

Failure to supply this information is an offence under s 154 of the Road Traffic Act 1988 and may result in prosecution by the police.

Please could you also confirm whether or not you are the registered keeper of the vehicle; if not, please supply the name and details of the person who is.

Yours

L4   Letter to the driver from the solicitor

This must be sent in all circumstances.

Dear

Our client:
Road accident date:
Location:

You were involved in a road traffic accident with our client on the above date.

We formally demand that you supply to us by return post confirmation that you were insured at the time of the accident, or confirmation that you would have been insured if your insurer had not avoided or cancelled your policy.

Please supply full details of your insurance policy including the following:

(a) The vehicle registration numbers covered by the policy of insurance.

(b) The policy number.

(c) The name of the insurer.

(d) The address of the insurer.

(e) The period of the insurance cover.

Please also supply a copy of the insurance policy.

If you were not insured at the time of the accident, please confirm this in writing.

Failure to supply this information is an offence under s 154 of the Road Traffic Act 1988 and may result in prosecution by the police.

Please could you also confirm whether or not you are the registered keeper of the vehicle; if not, please supply the name and details of the person who is.

Yours

L5 Letter to the police regarding failure to supply insurance policy details

This must be sent seven days after letters sent to the driver by the client and solicitor in the event of non-reply.

Police Station

BY FAX (for proof of sending)

Dear

Our client:
Road accident date:
Other driver's name:
Address:
Location of accident:

Our above-named client was involved in an accident with the above-named driver on the above date.

We have made a formal demand for insurance details from the driver in accordance with s 154 of the Road Traffic Act 1988 and have received no response.

As you are aware, it is an offence to fail to respond to our request and, in the circumstances, we would request that you investigate the matter and either obtain the details of insurance from the driver or prosecute the driver for failing to supply the information.

We attach a copy of our letters to the driver demanding the insurance details.

We thank you for your assistance.

Yours

L6   Letter to be sent with DVLA search form

To be sent in all circumstances where the registered keeper is unknown.

DVLA
Swansea
SA99 1BP

Direct dial:
Your ref:
Our ref: MIB/

Dear

Our client:
Road accident date:
Other driver's vehicle:

We are instructed by the above-named to pursue a claim for damages for personal injury, loss and expense as a result of a road traffic accident on the above date.

We enclose a completed DVLA search form. For the purpose of further investigating our client's claim, please confirm the name and address of the registered keeper of the vehicle at the time of the accident.

We enclose our cheque in settlement of the search fee.

Yours

L7   Letter to the registered keeper from the solicitor

This must be sent in all circumstances where the registered keeper is known.

Dear

Our client:
Road accident date:
Location:
Your vehicle:
Driver of your vehicle:

A vehicle of which you were the registered keeper was involved in a road traffic accident with our client on the above date.

We formally demand that you supply to us by return post confirmation that the vehicle was insured at the time of the accident, or confirmation that the vehicle would have been insured if your insurer had not avoided or cancelled your policy. This information is necessary irrespective of whether the driver concerned was insured under the policy.

Please supply full details of your insurance policy, including the following:

(a) The vehicle registration numbers covered by the policy of insurance.

(b) The policy number.

(c) The name of the insurer.

(d) The address of the insurer.

(e) The period of the insurance cover.

Please also supply a copy of the insurance policy.

Failure to supply this information is an offence under s 154 of the Road Traffic Act 1988 and may result in prosecution by the police.

If the vehicle was not insured at the time of the accident, please confirm this in writing.

If you were not the registered keeper of the vehicle at the time of the accident, please supply the name and details of the person who is and when you ceased to be the registered keeper.

Yours

L8 Letter to the police regarding the registered keeper's failure to provide details

This must be sent in all circumstances where the registered keeper is known and has failed to respond to the registered keeper.

BY FAX (for proof of sending)

Dear

Our client:
Road accident date:
Other driver's name:
Other vehicle:
Registered keeper:
Address:
Location of accident:

Our above-named client was involved in an accident with a vehicle. The details of the registered keeper are set out above.

We have made a formal demand for insurance details from the registered keeper in accordance with s 154 of the Road Traffic Act 1988 and have received no response.

As you are aware, it is an offence to fail to respond to our request and, in the circumstances, we would request that you investigate the matter and either obtain the details of insurance from the driver, or prosecute the driver for failing to supply the information.

We attach a copy of our letter to the driver demanding the insurance details. We have not received a response to this letter.

We thank you for your assistance.

Yours

4.4   CLIENT QUESTIONNAIRE

Q1 MIB Questionnaire

The MIB is a body set up to compensate victims of uninsured drivers. It is funded by a charge on all motor vehicle insurers. There are additional rules which apply to claims against the MIB, which can make it more difficult or even impossible to recover from the MIB. As a result, this additional questionnaire must be completed in order to ensure you receive compensation. If any documents or sections are missed, the MIB may be able to refuse to pay your compensation.

A	*'General Knowledge' Questions*	*Answer*
A	Were you travelling in the same vehicle as the driver who may have been uninsured at the time of the accident, or did you know the other driver? If no, please go to section F. If yes, please complete all further questions in this section.	
1	At the time of the accident, did you know that the driver was uninsured?	
2	If no, please state all the reasons why you thought the driver was (at the time of the accident) insured – include any knowledge that you have as to his driving record, his general character, his finances and other relevant information. (This is vitally important – please go on to a separate sheet if necessary.)	
3	At the time of the accident, did you think that the driver had a driving licence?	
4	If yes, why did you think that?	
5	Were you aware of any criminal or motoring convictions of the driver?	
6	If yes, please detail the knowledge that you had at the time of the accident.	

A	'General Knowledge' Questions	Answer
7	At the time of the accident, did you think that the driver was a disqualified driver?	
8	As far as you were aware at the time of the accident, who owned the vehicle in which you were travelling and who was the registered keeper?	
9	At the time of the accident, as far as you were aware, did the driver own any other vehicle?[26]	
10	Please describe the relationship between yourself and the driver – had you known him long?	
11	If you lived with the driver of the vehicle at the time of the accident, please confirm the following:[27]	
(A)	How long had you lived with the driver?	
(B)	Who purchased the vehicle in which you were a passenger at the time of the accident?	
(C)	Who arranged and paid for repairs, tax, maintenance, MOT tests, etc?	
(D)	Who was responsible for insuring the vehicle?	
(E)	Did you have joint or separate accounts?	
(F)	Who maintained the accounts, including who checked the statements, paid money into the account, etc?	

---

26 Questions 3 to 9 investigate the facts that determine whether or not the burden of proof shifts onto your client under Clause 6(3) – see 2.4.2.2 – such as your client being the owner or registered keeper.

27 The closer the relationship, the more likely it is that the MIB will argue that the passenger must have known whether the vehicle was insured or not.

A	'General Knowledge' Questions	Answer
(G)	Do you have insurance to drive the vehicle?	
12	Were you aware that the driver ever had to go to court and did you ask the circumstances? Please explain.[28]	
13	To your knowledge, had the driver had any previous accidents? If yes, had an insurance company paid for this damage or the damage caused to another vehicle?	
14	To your knowledge, had the driver ever been issued with a HORT1 (to produce his documents at the nearest police station)? Had he done so?	
15	To your knowledge, how long had the driver had access to the vehicle?	
16	Had you seen the driver driving other vehicles in the past? Roughly on how many occasions over what period of time?	
17	Were you aware of whether the driver drove vehicles as part of his employment?	

B	Additional Questions Where Vehicle was Stolen	Answer
B	Do you now know that the vehicle was stolen at the time of the accident? If yes, please complete the questions below; if no, please go on to section C.	

---

28 See *Cullen v Harman* (2000) unreported, 18 February.

B	Additional Questions Where Vehicle was Stolen	Answer
1	At the time of entering the vehicle, did you know that the vehicle was stolen?	
2	If no, at any time before the accident, did you become aware that the vehicle was stolen?	
3	If yes, after you discovered that the vehicle was stolen, did you have any opportunity to leave the vehicle from the time you discovered it was stolen to the time of the accident? If you did not, please give full details of any efforts you made and why you were not able to leave the vehicle.[29]	
4	Did you notice any damage to the vehicle, either outside or inside?	
5	If yes, was this damage indicative of theft?	
6	When in the vehicle, did you see how the driver started the vehicle? Did he have an ignition key? Where were you sitting in the vehicle?	
7	Who did you think the vehicle belonged to and why?	
8	Were you aware that the driver owned or had legitimate access to the vehicle or any other vehicles?	

29 This deals with the 'petrol station' defence (so called because if the driver stopped at a petrol station after your client had knowledge of the true state of affairs, then your client could have left the vehicle and therefore the MIB can refuse to satisfy the claim).

B	Additional Questions Where Vehicle was Stolen	Answer
9	Have you been convicted of an offence of being carried either in relation to this incident, or any other incident when the driver was driving?[30]	
10	To your knowledge, when you got into the vehicle, had the driver any previous convictions or been in trouble with the police? If yes, please give full details of what you knew.	

C	Drink and Drugs Questions	Answer
C	In cases where you were a passenger in the vehicle of the driver who may have been uninsured, do you now know that the driver was either under the influence of drink or drugs? If no, please go on to section D; if yes, please complete all questions in this section.	
1	How far over the alcohol limit was the driver (to your knowledge now)?[31]	
2	At the time of getting into the vehicle, did you think that the driver was over the limit? If no, how much did you think he had had to drink?	

---

30 Conviction for an offence of being carried entails knowledge by the defendant that the vehicle was stolen; such a conviction for the relevant incident would therefore preclude recovery of any damages. Proof of a previous conviction would entail knowledge that the driver has previously driven stolen cars, which would make any claim against the MIB very difficult.

31 The police accident report will usually assist with this information as it should contain statements as to the breath-test results at the police station – it should be checked, as if the driver was only just over the limit, the client has a far greater chance of convincing the court that he did not realise that the driver was over the limit.

C	Drink and Drugs Questions	Answer
3	Prior to getting into the vehicle, how much time had you spent with the driver out of the previous three or four hours?	
4	Had you seen him drink anything or take any form of drugs? If so, what and in what quantities?	
5	Do you know the driver well; did you know how he acted and behaved when drunk?	
6	Before you entered the vehicle, was there anything about the driver's behaviour or manner of his driving that alerted you to the fact that something was wrong?	
7	How was the driver behaving before entering the vehicle?	
8	Once you got into the vehicle and the journey commenced but prior to the accident, was there anything about the driver's behaviour, manner or driving that alerted you to the fact that he had been drinking/taking drugs?	
9	If yes, did you have an opportunity to leave the vehicle prior to the accident? What efforts did you make to leave and why could you not do so [see footnote 29 above]?	
10	Were you aware of the driver driving with excess alcohol before?	
11	Were you aware of the driver taking drugs before?	

D	Careless Driving Questions[32]	Answer
D	If you were a passenger in the vehicle driven by the driver who may have been uninsured, please complete all questions in this section.	
1	Had you driven with the driver before? If yes, give an estimate of the number of occasions.	
2	If you had driven with him before, was he normally a good or bad driver?	
3	Was the standard of the driver's driving poor (ie, speeding, swerving, dangerous, etc) on the journey on which the accident occurred prior to the actual accident?	
4	If yes, once you realised that the driver was driving dangerously, did you try to stop such driving or leave the vehicle [see footnote 29 above]? Please give details of what efforts you made and why they were unsuccessful.	

E	Other Criminal Conduct Questions	Answer
E	Were you travelling in the same vehicle as the driver who may have been uninsured at the time of the accident? Do you now know that the vehicle was being used in the course of or furtherance of a crime (other than driving whilst under the influence of drink or drugs, or dangerous or careless	

32 See 2.4.2.4 – knowledge that the vehicle was being used in the course or furtherance of a crime will exclude the MIB's liability. Dangerous driving and driving without due care and attention are crimes; however, the claim will not be excluded unless the MIB can show that the client knew the vehicle was going to be driven in this manner.

E	Other Criminal Conduct Questions	Answer
	driving)? Examples include vehicles which were being used to transport stolen goods or drugs, or carrying the driver or anyone else to or from the scene of a crime. If yes, please complete the further questions in this section.	
1	At the time of entering the vehicle, did you know that it was being used in the manner described above?	
2	What criminal conduct do you now know the vehicle was being used for? Please give full details including whether you or anyone else in the vehicle was arrested, and if so what for and what has subsequently happened.	

F	Questions to be Completed by All Clients	Answer
1	Did the accident occur in a place which was not a public road?[33]	
2	If yes, please give a full description of where the accident occurred, including whether the place at which it occurred was a place to which the general public had access. If the public had access, at what times of day and how many vehicles use the location where the accident occurred?	
3	Please give full details of what occurred at the scene of the accident, including any post-accident conversation that you had	

---

33 See 2.4.4 for the importance of such questions.

F	Questions to be Completed by All Clients	Answer
	with the other driver, including any questions you asked in relation to his insurance details and what his response was.[34]	
4	Please give full details of any subsequent communication you have had with the driver (or anyone acting on his behalf) in relation to whether he was insured at the time of the accident.	
5	Were the police called to the scene? If so, please give any details of who attended, from what police station, etc, and any subsequent dealings that you have had with them.	

I believe that the facts stated in this questionnaire are true.

Signed: ....

PRINT NAME: ....

Dated: ....

---

34 Although this should have been covered in the first interview in any event, it is wise to ensure that the client writes it down for you so you have a further source.

4.5   DIARY ENTRIES

DOCUMENT REFERENCE	DESCRIPTION	NUMBER OF DAYS
L2, L3 and L4	Letters sent to the client and to the driver from the client and solicitor	Immediately on receipt of instructions
	Telephone the driver within and outside office hours to ask for details of any insurer and for the details of the registered keeper	Immediately on receipt of instructions
	In the event of the client being the driver of another car, request the client's insurer to search the Motor Insurance Database to see if insurance details are evident	Immediately on receipt of instructions
L6	Letter and search form to DVLA for the registered keeper	Immediately on receipt of instructions
L5	If no insurance details supplied by the third party, send letter to police demanding they take action	7 days from letters L3 and L4 first being sent
L3 and L4	Duplicate letters to the driver from the client and solicitor if no response (add the time you will call the driver during an evening to give him the best chance of being available)[35]	14 days after L3 and L4 first sent
	Telephone the driver within and outside office hours (after having written to the driver advising him that you will call at a certain time) to ask for details of any insurer and for the details of the registered keeper, if no response last time	14 days after initial telephone enquiries
L2	Check response from the client has been received, the questionnaire has been completed and insurance policies provided; if no response, then send duplicate letter L2 and telephone to request that the client deals with it	14 days from letter L2 being sent

---

35   This will assist any future application for alternative service: see 6.3.1.

DOCUMENT REFERENCE	DESCRIPTION	NUMBER OF DAYS
	Chase response from the client's insurer search of the Motor Insurance Database	14 days from initial request being made
L7	Demand insurance details from the registered keeper of vehicle	As soon as details of registered keeper are known
L7	Duplicate demand sent to the registered keeper	7 days after L7 initially sent
L8	Complaint to police about failure to provide insurance details from the registered keeper	7 days after L7 initially sent
	If Motor Insurance Database search was initially carried out within three months of accident, request further search to be carried out (details of relevant policy may have been added)	42 days after Motor Insurance Database search completed

CHAPTER 5

PRE-ISSUE MATTERS

This chapter covers the practical steps that should be dealt with to put the claimant in the position of being able to issue proceedings well within the limitation period, in the event that the case is not settled earlier.

CHAPTER SUMMARY

5.1	**Attempt to settle claims at an early stage**	☐
5.2	**Maintain contact with the driver**	☐
5.3	**Complete the MIB application form**	☐
5.4	**Obtain documents for 'Proper Notice' bundle**	☐
5.4.1	Documents to be included	☐
5.5	**Documents**	☐
D3	Standard form for completion after discussion meeting	☐
5.6	**Standard letters**	☐
L9	Letter to the driver from the solicitor to be sent at various intervals prior to the expiry of the limitation period	☐
L10	Covering letter to the MIB enclosing application form and supporting documentation	☐
L11	Letter to the MIB requesting that it be added as a defendant and confirms other matters	☐
5.7	**CL2 Proper Notice checklist**	☐
5.8	**Diary entries**	☐

5.1   ATTEMPT TO SETTLE CLAIMS AT AN EARLY STAGE

Document D3

Most of the difficulties arising from MIB cases relate to the procedural hurdles that have to be overcome once proceedings have been issued. To reduce the likelihood of such difficulties potentially damaging the claimant's ability to obtain his rightful compensation, attempts should be made to settle such claims prior to the expiry of the limitation period. An early proactive approach to settlement, as envisaged and encouraged by the CPR in any event, will save costs in the long term, not least in insurance premiums if negligence claims are avoided.

Reviews of such files should be undertaken at least every 28 days (up until the issue of proceedings) and a proactive approach maintained; for instance, chasing GP's records, expert's reports, details from the claimant and their employer, etc. Early discussions with the MIB claims handler and ensuring that settlement meetings are arranged (either in person or over the telephone) should also progress the claim towards a consensual settlement rather than the approach of the expiry of the limitation period forcing the issue of proceedings.[1]

5.2   MAINTAIN CONTACT WITH THE DRIVER

Proceedings must still be issued against, and more importantly served upon, the uninsured driver if negotiations with the MIB do not succeed. Whilst an insurer will often nominate solicitors to accept service of proceedings to save having to serve the proceedings on their insured, the MIB is not in a position to do that as the defendant driver is not their insured. Attempts have to be made to trace the uninsured driver immediately after the first interview with the client and it is important to be certain that the name and address details that are obtained in relation to the uninsured driver are correct, at least at that stage.[2]

By the time that proceedings come to be issued and served, a couple of years may have passed. A diary entry should be made to check the current address of the third party driver 12 months prior to the expiry of the limitation period by the means highlighted below, and a further check should be made six months prior to the expiry date.[3]

Search name	Location	Comments
Send letter L9[4] to the driver which confirms his current address, asking him to sign it and return it in enclosed SAE		If it is signed and returned, then repeat in 6 months. If it is not returned within 28 days, then send duplicate, and then a further duplicate 14 days thereafter. If it is not returned or returned 'addressee

---

1   See 5.5, document D3, a standard form to be completed at the conclusion of such discussion meetings.
2   See 4.1.1.
3   See 5.6, letter L9.
4   See 5.6.

Search name	Location	Comments
		not known', then further steps should be taken
192.com	www.192.com	If a different address than already tried above is revealed, then send L9 to that address
DVLA search against the vehicle registration	DVLA Swansea, SA99 1BP	This will only reveal an up to date address if the vehicle still belongs to the same defendant. If address is revealed, then send L9 to that address
Experian	www.experian.com	Enquiries are made over the telephone to Experian (the date of birth of the uninsured driver is required). If you have the Experian disk, can do it on internet
Enquiry agent		If no replies are received from the L9 letters, then two calls should be made to the address on weekdays at reasonable hours, the second after a letter has been sent giving notice of the call. The agent should have with him the L9 letter so that the necessary signature can be obtained if the driver is in fact present

In the event of all these efforts proving unsuccessful, there should be sufficient evidence to enable a detailed witness statement to be drafted to support an application for service by an alternative means.[5]

---

5   See 6.3.1.

5.3 COMPLETE THE MIB APPLICATION FORM

Letters L10 and L11

Unless an MIB application form[6] with supporting information and documents is lodged, the MIB can refuse to deal with your client's claim. The forms are straightforward to complete. It is wise to lodge such an application form as early as possible to enable negotiations to commence. It must be lodged no later than 14 days after the commencement of proceedings.[7]

At the same time as lodging the MIB application form, together with the supporting documentation, a covering letter[8] should ask the MIB to confirm:

(1) that the application form complies with Clause 7 of the 1999 Agreement;[9]

(2) that the claim is accepted under the terms of the 1999 Agreement;[10]

(3) that the claim will be handled in accordance with the Revised Notes for Guidance 2002, concluded between the MIB, MASS, the Law Society and APIL;[11]

(4) that the MIB consents to be added as a defendant to the proceedings when proceedings are commenced.

If the application form has already been lodged without such a covering letter, or the letter acknowledging receipt of the application form does not specifically confirm the matters requested, then a further letter should be sent.[12]

When the application form is lodged, documents requested within the application form should be included; at the current time, these include copies of insurance policies for the benefit of your client[13] and the uninsured driver,

---

6 Application forms can be obtained from the MIB: see 1.6.2.

7 See Clause 5(3) of the Revised Notes for Guidance 2002, and also Clause 5(1), which allows 21 days from the date of proceedings where the claimant is not legally represented.

8 See 5.6, letter L10.

9 Once such confirmation is received, the MIB should be estopped from arguing that it did not comply at a later date.

10 This should prevent a later submission that an insurer should be dealing with the claim or that it should have proceeded under the Untraced Drivers Agreement.

11 These Notes for Guidance contain the agreement of the MIB to be joined as a second defendant and further, a number of concessions on notice requirements once they are joined as a second defendant. Such action removes the majority of the procedural difficulties and it is essential to establish that the MIB will deal with the claim in this way; again, it would be estopped from arguing that the Revised Notes for Guidance do not have binding authority once such a concession has been made.

12 See 5.6, letter L11.

13 See 4.1.8 for a list of what policies should be included.

along with the copy of correspondence with the driver, the registered keeper (if different) and any solicitor, insurer or agent connected to either of them.[14] The up to date application form should be checked to see what else is required.

5.4 OBTAIN DOCUMENTS FOR 'PROPER NOTICE' BUNDLE

When proceedings are issued, notice of issue to the MIB must be given within 14 days, enclosing the documents that constitute 'Proper Notice' as defined by Clause 9(2) of the Agreement, unless such documents were served with the application form under Clause 7. Such bundles should be prepared well in advance of the issue of proceedings, although some documents will have to be added once proceedings are issued.

The list below sets out the documents that should be obtained *prior* to the issue of proceedings.

5.4.1 Documents to be included

The checklist at 5.7 should be completed in all cases:

- Copies or details of any insurance policy providing benefits in the case of death, bodily injury or damage to property to which the proceedings relate where your client is the insured party and the benefits are available to him. See 4.1.8 for a list of which policies should be researched and the checklist at 5.7.

- Copies of all correspondence between your client and those acting (or who have acted) on his behalf, the driver and those acting (or who have acted) on his behalf, and the registered keeper (if known) and those acting (or who have acted) on his behalf. See 4.1.7 for suggested correspondence.

These documents do not have to be included if they were served with the application form (Clause 7). It is wise to check again the covering letter that was sent with the application form (letter L10) and examine the enclosures listed therein. Unless a letter has been received from the MIB, confirming that all enclosures listed were received by it, it is wise to send copies of these documents again.

---

14 Some of these documents have to be served in any event with the notice of issue of proceedings; see 5.4 on whether such documents have to be served again with notice of issue if already served with the application form.

5.5   DOCUMENTS

D3   Standard form for completion after discussion meeting

Client name: File ref:
Defendant name:
Accident date:

Those present:

Date: Times of meeting:

Discussions on liability (key issues):

Discussions on quantum:

Head of claim	Amount claimed	MIB offer	Agreed y/n?	Reasons

Interim payment agreed? £........... to be provided on or before .../.../200...

Further medical evidence agreed?

Expert:
Discipline:
Time limit:

Further comments:

Signed (acting on behalf of the claimant):

Signed (acting on behalf of the MIB):

5.6   STANDARD LETTERS

L9   Letter to the driver from the solicitor to be sent at various intervals prior to the expiry of the limitation period

Dear

Our client:
Road traffic accident date:
Location:

As you are aware, we are instructed to deal with a claim being made by our client in respect of a road traffic accident with you on the above date.

Please can you confirm that the address to which we have sent this letter is your current address and all the details are correct. In the event that this has been forwarded to you, that the address details are incorrect, or that you are changing address in the near future, please could you notify us. We enclose a stamped addressed envelope for your reply.

Yours

....

Driver's name:

Driver's address:

(Please delete as appropriate):

I confirm that the address details shown above are correct as of today's date.

Signed:

Date:

My address details have changed or will change as from .... and are/will be:

Address:

Signed:
Date:

L10 Covering letter to the MIB enclosing application form and supporting documentation

BY FAX:

Dear

Client name:
Accident date:
Uninsured driver:

We enclose a Motor Insurers' Bureau 1999 Uninsured Drivers Agreement ('the Agreement') application form. Please confirm that this complies with Clause 7 of 'the Agreement', and that you accept the claim under the terms of 'the Agreement'.

Please also confirm that the MIB will handle the claim in accordance with the 2002 Revised Notes for Guidance agreed, at the request of the Secretary of State for the Department of Transport, between the MIB, MASS, the Law Society and APIL, and will adhere to the amendments contained within those Revised Notes for Guidance where they differ from 'the Agreement', particularly the following points:

- where 'the Agreement' states that notices are to be given to the MIB within seven days, you will accept as good notice notice received within 14 days of the happening of the event;

- that the MIB agrees to be added as a defendant to the proceedings should proceedings subsequently become necessary; and

- where the MIB is added as a defendant to the proceedings from the commencement of the proceedings, the MIB will only require two notices in writing, namely:

  (a) notice in writing within 14 days of the date of issue of proceedings in accordance with Clause 9 of the 'the Agreement' (excluding Clause 9(3));

  (b) notice in writing within 14 days of the date of service of proceedings in accordance with Clause 10 of 'the Agreement'.

Please also confirm receipt of the enclosures listed below.

We enclose in support of the application the following information:

(1) Copies of insurance policies for the benefit of our client as follows.
   [*List all enclosures or insert 'None Applicable'*]

(2) Copies of correspondence between our client and those acting on his behalf and the uninsured driver, his solicitor, his insurers and those acting on his behalf.
[*List all enclosures or insert 'None Applicable'*]

(3) Copies/details of insurance policies for the benefit of the uninsured driver.
[*List all enclosures or insert 'None Applicable'*]

We await your response within 21 days.

Yours

L11 Letter to the MIB requesting that it be added as a defendant and confirm other matters

BY FAX:

Dear

Client name:
Accident date:
Uninsured driver:

We are proceeding with a claim under the 1999 Uninsured Drivers Agreement.

An application form has already been lodged with you. We will issue proceedings against the uninsured driver referred to above.

Please confirm the following within 14 days:

- the MIB will handle the claim in accordance with the 2002 Revised Notes for Guidance agreed, at the request of the Secretary of State for the Department of Transport, between the MIB, MASS, the Law Society and APIL, and will adhere to the amendments contained within those Revised Notes for Guidance where they differ from the 1999 Uninsured Drivers Agreement, particularly on the following points:

  (a) that where the Agreement states that notices are to be given to the MIB within seven days, it will accept as good notice notice received within 14 days of the happening of the event;

  (b) that the MIB agrees to be added as a defendant to the proceedings;

  (c) that where the MIB is added as a defendant to the proceedings from the commencement of the proceedings, the MIB will only require two notices in writing, namely:

    (i) notice in writing within 14 days of the date of issue of proceedings in accordance with Clause 9 of the Agreement (excluding Clause 9(3));

    (ii) notice in writing within 14 days of the date of service of proceedings in accordance with Clause 10 of the Agreement.

Should an insurer subsequently be located, please treat this as notice pursuant to s 152 of the Road Traffic Act 1988 that proceedings will be issued.

Yours

5.7 CL2 PROPER NOTICE CHECKLIST

Document	Request to client (date)	Obtained from client (date)	No such document in existence – confirmed (date)	Sent with application form (Yes/No)	Copied and placed on Proper Notice bundle file (date)	To be prepared pre-issue (Yes/No)
Insurance Documents: (Clause 9(2)(c))						
Vehicle insurance policy						Yes
Private healthcare insurance policy						Yes
Household insurance policy						Yes
Credit card policies						Yes
Legal expense insurance policy						Yes
Employers' insurance						Yes
Union benefits policy						Yes
Personal accident insurance cover						Yes
Any other insurance policy that the claimant can benefit from						Yes
Correspondence documents: (Clause 9(2)(d))						
Copy of all correspondence between the claimant and the driver/registered keeper						Yes

Document	Request to client (date)	Obtained from client (date)	No such document in existence – confirmed (date)	Sent with application form (Yes/No)	Copied and placed on Proper Notice bundle file (date)	To be prepared pre-issue (Yes/No)
Copy of all correspondence between the claimant's solicitor and the driver/registered keeper						Yes
Copy of all correspondence between the previous solicitor/accident management claims firm and the driver/registered keeper						Yes
Copy of all correspondence between the driver/registered keeper and anyone else acting for the claimant						Yes
Copy of all correspondence between the client/any person acting for him and any person acting on behalf of the driver/registered keeper						Yes
Notice provisions: (Clauses 9(2)(a), 9(2)(b), 9(2)(e))						
Notice in writing that proceedings commenced by claim form, writ or other means	N/A	N/A	N/A	N/A		No
Sealed claim form or writ	N/A	N/A	N/A	N/A		No

Sealed particulars of claim[15]	N/A	N/A	N/A	N/A	No
Notice of issue of proceedings[16]					
Such other information about the relevant proceedings as the MIB may reasonably specify (Clause 9(2)(g))[17]					
Copies of all other documents which should be served on a defendant with the claim form/ particulars of claim: (Clause 9(2)(f))					
Medical reports	N/A	N/A	N/A	N/A	Yes
Schedule of special damage	N/A	N/A	N/A	N/A	Yes
Documents in support of schedule of special damage	N/A	N/A	N/A	N/A	Yes
Notice of funding (CFA/LSC)	N/A	N/A	N/A	N/A	Yes
The response pack[18]	N/A	N/A	N/A	N/A	No

15 If proceedings are issued without the particulars of claim being served, the particulars of claim do not have to be served until seven days after service on the defendant. However, it is advisable to serve the particulars with the claim form to avoid the additional notice of service of the particulars of claim. **NB:** Clause 9(2)(f) states that Proper Notice includes service on the MIB of all documents required to be served with the claim form and particulars of claim. No exception is allowed if the particulars of claim are not served on the defendant with the claim form; therefore, the schedule of special damages (with supporting documentation), medical evidence, notice of funding and response pack must still be served on the MIB, even if the particulars of claim are not.

16 Clause 9(2)(b): 'a copy of the sealed claim form, writ or other official document providing evidence of the commencement of the proceedings'. In *Cambridge v Callaghan* (1997) The Times, 21 March, the plaint note (now notice of issue) was deemed to be a document initiating the proceedings.

17 Check correspondence to ensure that the MIB has not requested additional documentation to be disclosed to them with Proper Notice. If the request is unreasonable, refer to the Secretary of State (Clause 19). See Chapter 7.

18 The Revised Notes for Guidance 2002 provide that it is not necessary to include this. See 2.5.

5.8   DIARY ENTRIES

Document reference	Description	Number of days
	General review of file	Every 28 days
L10 and application form	Covering letter to be sent, accompanied by fully completed application form	As soon as information required is available; review every 28 days until done
	Check whether the MIB has answered L10 and confirmed all details requested. Send chasing letter with duplicate letter, forms and documents enclosed if necessary	Every 28 days until done
	Consider whether settlement meeting appropriate to discuss either liability or quantum	Every 6 months
L9	Letter to the driver to confirm current address details	12 months prior to the limitation expiry date
L9	Duplicate letter if no reply to first letter	28 days after L9 originally sent
L9	Duplicate letter if no reply to second letter	14 days after second L9 sent
	If no reply to any of L9 letters, take steps as set out in table at 5.2	14 days after third L9 sent
L9	Letter to the driver to confirm current address details (if original letter was answered)	6 months prior to the limitation expiry date
L9	Duplicate letter if no reply to first letter	28 days after L9 originally sent
L9	Duplicate letter if no reply to second letter	14 days after second L9 sent
	If no reply to any of the L9 letters, take steps as set out in table at 5.2	14 days after third L9 sent

Document reference	Description	Number of days
CL2	Chase outstanding items and complete all pre-issue steps in checklist	6 months prior to the expiry of the limitation period and then review every 28 days until done
L11	Check whether the MIB has confirmed agreement to be joined as a defendant; if not, send L11	6 months prior to the expiry of the limitation period and then repeat every 28 days until response is received

CHAPTER 6

ISSUING PROCEEDINGS

This chapter deals with all the steps that need to be taken when proceedings are issued. It is worth remembering that many professional negligence claims arise because of a failure to undertake the procedural steps that are necessary.

If proceedings are issued and you subsequently realise that the correct procedural steps were not followed, it is important that you obtain clear, unequivocal written confirmation that the MIB will not rely on the point (effectively that it will waive the point) and if not (if the claim is still within limitation), that you immediately discontinue and reissue the claim, undertaking the correct procedural steps.

CHAPTER SUMMARY

6.1	**Joining the MIB as a second defendant**	☐
6.2	**Issuing the proceedings**	☐
6.3	**Service on the defendant**	☐
6.3.1	Application for service by alternative means	☐
6.4	**Service on the MIB**	☐
6.5	**Notices to the MIB**	☐
6.5.1	Notice of issue of the proceedings	☐
6.5.2	Notice of service of the proceedings on the defendant	☐
6.5.2.1	Notice of the deemed date of service	☐
6.5.2.2	Notice of the date of personal service of the proceedings	☐
6.5.2.3	Notice of the date the defendant confirms service of the proceedings upon him	☐
6.5.2.4	Notice of the date the claimant receives confirmation from the court that service of the proceedings has occurred	☐
6.5.2.5	Notice of service of the proceedings on the MIB	☐
6.6	**Documents**	☐
D4	Draft particulars of claim	☐
D5	Draft witness statement for an application for service by alternative method	☐
D6	Record of fax to the MIB	☐
6.7	**Standard letters**	☐
L12	Letter to the court for issue of proceedings against the MIB	☐

L13	Letter to the claimant advising of the issue of proceedings	☐
L14	Letter serving proceedings on the defendant	☐
L15	Letter to the MIB serving proceedings/notice of service/ notice of intention to apply for judgment	☐
L16	Letter to the MIB giving notice of personal service of proceedings	☐
L17	Letter to the MIB giving notice of confirmation of service on the defendant	☐
6.8	**Diary entries**	☐

6.1   JOINING THE MIB AS A SECOND DEFENDANT

In the Revised Notes for Guidance 2002, it states that: 'When it is decided to commence legal proceedings, the MIB should be joined as a defendant (unless there is a good reason not to do so).' The MIB's agreement to such a course of action should have been confirmed prior to issue (see letter L11 at 5.6 if not already sent).

The wording which should be used in the particulars of claim is set out in the aforesaid Notes for Guidance and incorporated into the draft particulars of claim set out at 6.6.

It is important to join the MIB as a second defendant, as the revised Notes for Guidance 2002 state that where this is done (because the court will then inform the MIB of various steps in proceedings), some of the later (onerous) notice requirements in the 1999 Agreement do not have to be complied with. However, *this does not include the notice of issue or notice of service.*

If the MIB is joined as a second defendant, the proceedings should be served on the registered office.[1]

6.2   ISSUING THE PROCEEDINGS

```
Letter L12
```

The documents required to be served on the MIB with the notice of issue should have been prepared already.[2] Ensure that you have prepared sufficient copies of the claim form, particulars of claim, medical evidence, schedule, etc, in order that you have copies for:

---

1   See 1.6.2.
2   See 5.4.

(1) the court;

(2) the defendant;

(3) the MIB and any nominated solicitor;

(4) any potential insurer;

(5) your file;

(6) one spare.

When all the copies are prepared, they should be taken by hand to your local court for issue.[3] Your local court should be used so that you can collect the notice of issue. On no account should the court ever be requested to issue and serve the proceedings as, if you subsequently discover that they have managed to serve the defendant, the time limit for notifying the MIB of this fact may have already expired.

If the court will not issue proceedings whilst an employee waits, daily telephone calls should be made to establish whether proceedings have been issued. Despite the fact that the letter L12 specifically requests that you are notified as soon as proceedings have been issued and the proceedings are not to be served on the defendant, if the court makes a mistake and does so, the MIB could still avoid liability.

If an insurer may have been in any way involved in the proceedings, a s 152 notice should be provided to them. A copy of the proceedings can be sent with the notice. If the MIB has nominated solicitors to accept service, remember that the proceedings must then be served on the solicitors, otherwise they are not effectively served. Serve an additional copy on the MIB for the sake of completeness.

At the same time as proceedings are issued, the claimant should be warned of the importance of notifying you of any contact from the defendant. Send standard letter L13 to the claimant (see 6.7).

6.3   SERVICE ON THE DEFENDANT

Letter L14

As set out at 5.2, the uninsured driver (defendant) must be served with the proceedings[4] and therefore various steps should have been taken to maintain contact with him. In the event, however, that, by the time service of proceedings

---

3   See 6.7, letter L12.

4   See 6.7, letter L14.

arises, this proves impossible, an application for service by alternative means (on the MIB) can be made[5] once service has been tried and failed.

6.3.1 Application for service by alternative means

Document D5

Such an application (which should be made on the standard form N244) should be made after the issue of proceedings once attempts to serve the defendant uninsured driver have proved unsuccessful, and should be supported by a witness statement.[6]

Before the application is made, a copy of the correspondence, enquiry agent's report and all other attempts to locate and serve the defendant should be sent to the MIB or its solicitors, requesting that it consents to an order for alternative service on the defendant by serving the MIB. A response should be requested within 14 days, and if a positive response is not received, the necessary application should be issued. In most cases where you have made an effort to serve the proceedings, the MIB will consent to such an application, in which case, a consent application can be made.

A draft witness statement is set out at 6.6 (document D5). If you have attempted to maintain contact with the defendant as detailed in 5.2, but have discovered that the address you hold is not the current address, the application should be made soon after the issue of proceedings, and should be accompanied with an application for an extension of time for service from the standard four months.

---

5 See *Clarke v Vedel* [1979] RTR 26, in which Stephenson LJ, giving judgment in the Court of Appeal, stated that 'there may be cases where a defendant, who cannot be traced and, therefore, is unlikely to be reached by any form of substituted service, can nevertheless be ordered to be served at the address of the insurers or the Bureau in a road accident case. The existence of insurers and the Bureau and of these various agreements does create a special position which enables the plaintiff to avoid the strictness of the general rule and obtain such an order for substituted service in some cases'.

6 See CPR, r 6.8, Pt 6, PD para 9.1, and document D5. The Rule states that where there appears to the court to be a good reason to authorise service by a method not permitted by these Rules, the court may make an order permitting service by an alternative method. An application for an order permitting service by an alternative method must be supported by evidence and may be made without notice (for obvious reasons). The Practice Direction states that the evidence should state the reason why an alternative method of service is sought and what steps have been taken to serve by other means.

6.4   SERVICE ON THE MIB

In the 1999 Agreement, Clause 8 states that:

> [A]ny notice required to be given or documents to be supplied to the MIB pursuant to Clauses 9 to 12 of this Agreement shall be sufficiently given or supplied only if sent by facsimile transmission or by Registered or Recorded Delivery post to the MIB's registered office for the time being and delivery shall be proved by the production of a facsimile transmission report produced by the sender's facsimile machine or an appropriate postal receipt.

Therefore, the notice of relevant proceedings, together with the documents set out in the checklist, as well as further notices set out in Chapter 7, have to be served by fax or recorded or registered delivery.[7] The 2002 Revised Notes for Guidance (and these should only be relied upon if the MIB has confirmed in writing that it will deal with the claim under those Revised Notes and then only subject to 2.5) state that if the claimant proves service by DX, first class post, personal service or any other form of service accepted by the Civil Procedure Rules, the MIB will accept that such notice has been served in the same circumstances as any party under the CPR would be obliged to accept valid service. It is still probably worth serving those matters set out in 6.3 by fax or recorded delivery post, to ensure compliance with the Agreement, however; in that way, no later disputes can arise.

When sending notice by fax, it is advisable for the fee-earner to send the fax to ensure all pages are sent. If there is any dispute as to whether notice was given, fully or at all, it should be the fee-earner giving the evidence. A fax sheet is included at 6.6, document D6, which should always be completed, as it would be a useful exhibit to a statement if there is any dispute as to effective service.

An immediate telephone call should be made by the person who sent the fax to confirm that the MIB has received it. A further telephone call should be made three days later, to confirm receipt of the proceedings. Obtain the name and position of the person confirming receipt of the notice and ensure that all the enclosures listed were received. A full and detailed attendance note should be made to ensure that there can be no dispute at a later date.

6.5   NOTICES TO THE MIB

6.5.1   Notice of issue of the proceedings

> Checklist CL2, letter L15

The claimant *must* give proper notice of the bringing of the relevant proceedings no later than 14 days from the commencement of proceedings,

---

7   Registered delivery has now been replaced by Special Delivery. As this is not yet specified in the Agreement as an authorised means of service on the MIB, it is sensible to only serve by fax or recorded delivery.

irrespective of whether the MIB is joined as a second defendant. It does not matter whether or not the MIB is aware of the intention to bring proceedings; it must be given notice that proceedings have been issued. The time limit runs from the date proceedings are in fact issued by the court, NOT from when the claimant (or his solicitor) becomes aware that they have been issued.[8] If notice is given outside the notice period, the MIB can say nothing until limitation has expired and then rely on this point to avoid satisfying the judgment.[9] Therefore, if a time limit has been missed or another breach has occurred, unless the MIB provides written, unequivocal confirmation that the breach will not be relied upon at a later date, the solicitor should discontinue and reissue proceedings prior to limitation expiring.

The notice of issue must include notice in writing that proceedings have been commenced by claim form or writ (the notice of issue), together with a copy of the sealed claim form or writ.[10] There are a number of other documents that should be included to ensure proper notice is given; refer to the checklist at 5.7, and ensure that each document is included, unless (in the case of the insurance policies and correspondence) it was included with the application form. A standard letter (L15) is included at 6.7 to accompany the notice of issue. This also includes notice of the deemed date of service on the defendant[11] and notice of intention to apply for judgment.[12] Even if you choose not to serve the particulars of claim with the claim form, you must still disclose the documents required to be served with the particulars of claim with the notice of issue of proceedings.[13]

---

8   See for instance *Silverton v Goodall* [1997] PIQR 451, where, in a case under the 1988 Agreement, the claimant's solicitors did not give the MIB the requisite notice of issue within the relevant time period and served it late, because the court did not send the notice to the claimant's solicitors until after that time period had expired (due to unexplained delays in the court office). The claimant's solicitors subsequently joined the MIB as a defendant, and that claim was struck out due to their failure to comply with the notice period. The Court of Appeal upheld that decision.

9   See for instance *Wake v Wylie* [2001] RTR 20; [2001] PIQR 13, a case concerning incorrect notice given to s 151 insurers where the claimant's solicitors were held not to have given proper notice of the bringing of proceedings. The Court of Appeal held that there had been no representation on the insurers' part that might found a claim based on estoppel; it was open to the insurers to wait until judgment had been entered against the driver and recovery then sought from them before arguing that the notice provisions had not been complied with, and therefore the point had not been waived. The same arguments would seem to apply if the case had concerned the MIB.

10 See for instance *Cambridge v Callaghan* (1997) The Times, 21 March, where the Court of Appeal held that the MIB did not have to satisfy a judgment where a copy of an unstamped writ or notice of issue was served.

11 Clause 10(3)(b): see 6.5.2.1.

12 Clause 12: see 7.1.5.

13 Clause 9(2)(f) states that 'Proper Notice' includes service on the MIB of all documents required to be served with the claim form and the particulars of claim. No exception is allowed if the particulars of claim are not served on the defendant with the claim form; therefore, the schedule of special damages (with supporting documentation), medical evidence, notice of funding and the response pack must still be served on the MIB, even if the particulars of claim are not.

6.5.2   Notice of service of the proceedings on the defendant

The claimant must give notice of service of the proceedings to the MIB within seven days of the following circumstances:

(1) the date of personal service of the proceedings;

(2) the date the defendant confirms service of the proceedings upon him;

(3) the date the claimant receives confirmation from the court that service of the proceedings has occurred; or

(4) within 14 days of the deemed date of service.

6.5.2.1   Notice of the deemed date of service

> ### Letter L15

Notice of the deemed date of service is included with the notice of issue of proceedings to the MIB (6.7, letter L15). If it is not given with the notice of issue it must be given within 14 days of the deemed date of service.

6.5.2.2   Notice of the date of personal service of the proceedings

> ### Letter L16

If proceedings are served personally, any doubt as to the date or validity of service is instantly removed. The date, time and location of service are all known as soon as service has been effected. If the server cannot locate the defendant, you will receive early notification that an application for service by an alternative method is required.[14] Notice can be given to the MIB that personal service has been effected as soon as confirmation is received from the server (see 6.7, letter L16).

6.5.2.3   Notice of the date the defendant confirms service of the proceedings upon him

> ### Letters L13 and L17

It may seem unlikely that the defendant will confirm service of the proceedings to the claimant or his solicitors. However, this is more likely to happen than

---

14   See 6.3.1.

might at first be considered. It is best demonstrated by examples as it is one of the more difficult notices with which to comply:

(1) The defendant, furious at receiving a claim form blaming him for the accident, telephones the claimant or visits him at his home address given on the claim form, and protests. If this happens, there are seven days in which to tell the MIB that the defendant has received the claim form. Therefore, the claimant must be warned when proceedings are served that if the defendant contacts him, he must telephone his solicitor immediately.[15]

(2) The defendant, furious at receiving a claim form blaming him for the accident, telephones the solicitor's office to protest. He speaks to a secretary while the fee-earner is on holiday. He does not ask for a return call as he has just telephoned to vent his anger. The secretary files the attendance note. Notice of service to the MIB within seven days is not given; therefore, if no other notice of service has been given, the MIB can now reject the claim.

It is easy for this notice to be missed, which is why the file must be checked regularly after the service of proceedings (at, say, three day intervals) to ensure no such telephone calls are received. It is another reason for a dedicated MIB team (see 3.1).

6.5.2.4 Notice of the date the claimant receives confirmation from the court that service of the proceedings has occurred

The court should never be allowed to issue and serve proceedings in MIB cases. See 6.2. Therefore, this notice should not be required to be given to the MIB.

6.5.2.5 Notice of service of the proceedings on the MIB

When the MIB is added as a defendant to the proceedings, notice must be given to the MIB within seven days of service of the proceedings on it. This is provided for by the terms of the 1999 Agreement (Clause 10).[16]

---

15 See letters L13 (to the claimant) and L17 (to the MIB).
16 See 6.7, letter L15.

6.6   DOCUMENTS

D4   Draft particulars of claim

IN THE [TOWN] COUNTY COURT

BETWEEN: **Claim no**

ADAM CLAIMANT

Claimant

And

EVE DEFENDANT

First defendant

And

THE MOTOR INSURERS' BUREAU

Second defendant

PARTICULARS OF CLAIM

(1) On 1 December 2000, the claimant was driving his motor vehicle, registration number A123 XXX, along the A38 in a southbound direction between Xtown and Ytown when the first defendant, who was driving his motor vehicle, registration number B456 YYY, in the opposite direction, negligently crossed into the claimant's carriageway and a collision occurred.

(2) The aforesaid accident was caused by the first defendant's negligence in that he:

PARTICULARS OF NEGLIGENCE

(a) crossed the central white line into the opposing carriageway;

(b) failed to heed the presence of the claimant's motor vehicle correctly proceeding towards him;

(c) failed to keep any or any adequate look out;

(d) failed to control his motor vehicle so as to ensure it remained on the correct carriageway;

(e) failed in the circumstances to take reasonable care for the claimant's safety.

(3) As a result of the accident, the claimant sustained personal injury, loss and damage [particularise as usual].

(4) The second defendant is a company limited by guarantee under the Companies Act. Pursuant to an Agreement with the Secretary of State for the Environment, Transport and the Regions dated 13 August 1999, the

second defendant provides compensation in certain circumstances to persons suffering injury or damage as a result of the negligence of uninsured motorists.

(5) The claimant has used all reasonable endeavours to ascertain the liability of an insurer for the first defendant and at the time of the commencement of these proceedings verily believes that the first defendant is not insured.

(6) The claimant accepts that only if a final judgment is obtained against the first defendant (which judgment is not satisfied in full within seven days from the date upon which the claimant became entitled to enforce it) can the second defendant be required to satisfy the judgment and then only if the terms and conditions set out in the Agreement are satisfied. Until that time, any liability of the second defendant is only contingent.

(7) To avoid the second defendant having later to apply to join itself to this action (which the claimant must consent to in any event, pursuant to Clause 14(b) of the Agreement), the claimant seeks to include the second defendant from the outset, recognising fully the second defendant's position as reflected in (4) above and the rights of the second defendant fully to participate in the action to protect its position as a separate party to the action.

(8) With the above in mind, the claimant seeks a declaration of the second defendant's contingent liability to satisfy the claimant's judgment against the first defendant.

(9) Further, the claimant claims interest pursuant to section 69 of the County Court Act 1984 [particularise as usual].

D5 Draft witness statement for an application for service by alternative method (Civil Procedure Rules, Rule 6.8, Pt 6, PD para 9.1)

IN THE [TOWN] COUNTY COURT

Insert usual statement details
in top right hand corner

BETWEEN:

Claim no

ADAM CLAIMANT

Claimant

And

EVE DEFENDANT

First defendant

And

THE MOTOR INSURERS' BUREAU

Second defendant

I [name, address and description] state that:

(1) Having been instructed by the [claimant/claimant's solicitor] to serve the first defendant with a copy of the claim form in these proceedings, which has been duly sealed with the seal of the Issuing Court and accompanied by the response pack, on [date] I attended for the purpose of serving a copy of those documents on the first defendant at [address].

(2) [In this paragraph, the full attempts to effect service should be detailed. Any correspondence sent to the defendant's address should be exhibited (see Chapter 5), as well as any reply; any attempts to trace a different address should be detailed, and then any attempts to effect service, which should be at least two attempts at personal attendance at the address in question – unless the first attendance led to an unequivocal answer that the defendant was no longer living there and left no forwarding address.]

(3) I believe that I have made all reasonable efforts and used all means in my power to serve the claim form and response pack, but I have not been able to do so. I ask for an order for service by the following alternative method, namely service upon the second defendant, the Motor Insurers' Bureau.

(4) I believe that the facts stated in this witness statement are true.

Signed and dated, etc

D6   Record of fax to the MIB

FAX SHEET

Fax addressed to:	
Fax number sent to:	
Date of fax:	
Time of fax:	
Enclosures faxed (please detail):	
Enclosures checked against those detailed in covering letter and all included:	
Name of person sending fax:	
Signature of person sending fax:	
Total number of pages sent:	
Fax transmission report attached:	
Copy of covering letter attached:	Date: Addressee:

6.7   STANDARD LETTERS

L12   Letter to the court for issue of proceedings against the MIB

The Chief Clerk

County court

BY HAND

SOLICITOR TO SERVE ON the MIB and the DEFENDANT – PLEASE ISSUE AND RETURN IMMEDIATELY

Dear

………. v …………. and Motor Insurers' Bureau

We enclose the following:

(1) Claim form (x6).
(2) Particulars of claim (x6).
(3) Supporting medical evidence (x6).
(4) Schedule of special damages (x6).
(5) [Notice of funding form.]
(6) Issue fee of £……..

Please issue proceedings and return all spare sealed copies of the proceedings to us, along with the response pack and notice of issue, for service on the MIB and the defendant. We have enclosed additional copies for sealing as the claim involves the MIB and the procedure is more complicated.

Please note that the MIB is involved in proceedings. As notice must be given to it as soon as proceedings have been issued, and no later than 14 days after issue, we would be grateful if you would issue proceedings while our employee waits. If you are not able to do this, please call *(insert number)* once the papers have been sealed and we will arrange to collect them.

Please also note that once proceedings are issued, the claimant has numerous obligations to meet before he can obtain compensation from the MIB. If any document which the claimant would normally receive from the court is filed at court by the defendant, the MIB, or any other party to the proceedings, the claimant may have to advise the MIB of this event within seven days of the court receiving the communication. Failure to do so may result in the claimant receiving no compensation and also to a potential negligence claim. In the circumstances, we would ask that any such communications are forwarded on to us on the date of receipt by the court.

We would also ask that the court should not enter judgment of its own motion. The MIB requires 35 days' notice of any intention to apply for judgment.

Yours

L13   Letter to the claimant advising of the issue of proceedings

To be sent in all cases.

Dear

Road accident date:
Other driver's name:

Proceedings are now being issued by the court against the above-named driver. As you are aware, your claim is finally likely to be paid by the MIB. To ensure any judgment obtained against the other driver is paid by the MIB, you must comply with certain requirements, or the MIB can avoid paying compensation to you.

If you receive any contact from the other driver, or the registered keeper of the vehicle if that is someone else, you must immediately notify me, however trivial the contact might seem, and whether in writing, on the telephone or through a face to face meeting. Failure to do so may result in the MIB being able to avoid paying you any compensation.

Please acknowledge receipt of this letter.

Yours

L14   Letter serving proceedings on the defendant

Dear

.... v .... and Motor Insurers' Bureau

We are instructed by the claimant in these proceedings to recover compensation for injuries, losses and expenses sustained following a road traffic accident.

We enclose by way of service the following:

(1) Copy of the sealed claim form.
(2) Particulars of claim.
(3) Medical reports of ...... dated ......
(4) Schedule of special damages with supporting documentation.
(5) Notice of funding.
(6) Response pack, including a form for defending the claim, a form for admitting the claim and a form for acknowledging service.

In view of the fact that you were uninsured, the Motor Insurers' Bureau is also involved in the proceedings. If you did hold a policy of insurance at the time of the accident, or had the benefit of a policy of insurance at the time of the accident, you must notify us immediately, supplying full details.

Please acknowledge receipt of this letter.

Yours

L15 Letter to the MIB serving proceedings/notice of service/notice of intention to apply for judgment

Motor Insurers' Bureau

[Registered Office]

BY FAX AND RECORDED DELIVERY:

Dear

Claimant:
Defendant/uninsured driver:
Defendant's/uninsured driver's address:
Accident date:
County court:
Claim no:
Date proceedings issued:
Date proceedings served by first class post on defendant:[17]
Deemed date of service:
Date proceedings served by first class post on the MIB:[18]
Deemed date of service:

We give you notice of issue of proceedings in the above matter and we also give you notice of deemed service as detailed above. We also confirm that if the defendant does not file a defence in these proceedings, on or after 35 days from today's date, we will apply to the court for default judgment.

We enclose by way of service the following:

(1) Copy of the sealed claim form.

(2) Particulars of claim (served on the defendant with the claim form).

(3) Medical reports of .... dated ....

(4) Schedule of special damages with supporting documentation.

(5) [Notice of funding.][19]

(6) [Response pack.][20]

(7) Copies of insurance contracts for the benefit of the claimant as detailed below:
     [List each and every insurance policy included, using the checklist at 5.7]

---

17 See 6.5.2.1.

18 See 6.5.2.5.

19 Those matters in square brackets may be unnecessary.

20 See footnotes to checklist at 5.7 as to whether this is necessary.

(8) [Copies/details of insurance policies for the benefit of the defendant.]

(9) Copies of correspondence between the claimant, or those acting on his behalf, and the defendant, or those acting on his behalf [and the defendant's insurers], and listed below.
   [List each and every piece of correspondence included, using the checklist at 5.7]

(10) Letter dated *(insert date)* serving the proceedings on the first defendant.

This letter constitutes Proper Notice under Clause 9 of the Uninsured Drivers Agreement 1999, notice of service of the claim form pursuant to Clause 10 and notice of intention to apply for judgment pursuant to Clause 12.

Please acknowledge receipt by return.

Yours

L16 Letter to the MIB giving notice of personal service of proceedings

Motor Insurers' Bureau
[Registered Office]

BY FAX AND RECORDED DELIVERY:

Dear

Claimant:
Claim no:
Date of personal service:

We confirm that personal service of the claim form was effected on the defendant on the above date.

We enclose a copy of the Statement of Service.

Please confirm receipt of this notice of personal service pursuant to Clause 10(3)(iii) by return.

Yours

L17 Letter to the MIB giving notice of confirmation of service on the defendant

Motor Insurers' Bureau
[Registered Office]

BY FAX AND RECORDED DELIVERY:

Dear

Claimant:
Claim no:
Date of confirmation of service by the defendant:

We confirm that on the above date we received notification that service of the claim form had taken place.

We enclose a copy of the Notice of Acknowledgment of Service, letter from the defendant/Solicitors/Insurers/Agent – *delete as appropriate.*

Please confirm receipt of this notice of service pursuant to Clause 10(3)(ii) by return.

Yours

6.8   DIARY ENTRIES

DOCUMENT REFERENCE	DESCRIPTION	NUMBER OF DAYS TO REVIEW
L11	Check agreement of the MIB to be joined as a second defendant	Fax duplicate L11 if not already obtained agreement
L12	Take all documents to local court by hand and request issue of proceedings	
L13	Send letter to the client warning of the importance of notifying you of any contact from the defendant	3 days from L12
L13	Telephone client if no response received to L13	7 days from L13
	If sealed copies not provided immediately, ring the court and request whether they have been sealed; if they have, collect immediately	Following day from delivery of documents to the court and thereafter every working day until sealed documents are received
L14, L15	Serve on the defendant (and the MIB if joined as a second defendant)	Within 1 working day of collection of sealed documents
L15	Send the MIB notice of issue (and all other documentation) by fax	Within 1 working day of collection of sealed documents **NB**: the MIB *must* receive notice of issue within 14 days of the date of issue
D6	Complete fax transmission report for service on the MIB – ensure telephone call made to confirm fax has been received	Same day as fax is sent

DOCUMENT REFERENCE	DESCRIPTION	NUMBER OF DAYS TO REVIEW
	Telephone the MIB requesting confirmation that notice has been received and all enclosures listed within covering letter have been received	3 days after fax is sent – repeat daily if person is unable to confirm
	Check that the MIB has confirmed that notice has been received. In the event that there is any danger that the deadline may be missed, proceedings will have to be reissued	12 days after issue of proceedings – if not, chase
L17	Check file for any confirmation of service from the defendant (6.5.2.3)	3 days after proceedings are deemed to be served on the defendant – repeat daily

CHAPTER 7

PROCEEDINGS POST-ISSUE

CHAPTER SUMMARY

7.1	**Notice requirements**	☐
7.1.1	Service of the particulars of claim	☐
7.1.2	Filing of the defence	☐
7.1.2.1	By the defendant	☐
7.1.2.2	By the MIB	☐
7.1.3	Amendment to the particulars of claim/documents required to be served therewith	☐
7.1.3.1	The claim form	☐
7.1.3.2	The particulars of claim	☐
7.1.3.3	The schedule of special damage and loss	☐
7.1.3.4	Medical reports	☐
7.1.3.5	The notice of funding	☐
7.1.3.6	Amendment by another claimant to the proceedings	☐
7.1.3.7	Revised Notes for Guidance 2002	☐
7.1.4	Trial date applied for or fixed by the court (seven days)	☐
7.1.4.1	Allocation or listing questionnaire filed by the claimant	☐
7.1.4.2	Allocation directions issued by the court including a warned period or fixed date for the trial	☐
7.1.4.3	The court fixes a date for the trial after filing of listing questionnaires	☐
7.1.4.4	Revised Notes for Guidance 2002	☐
7.1.5	Application for judgment (35 days)	☐
7.1.5.1	Revised Notes for Guidance 2002	☐
7.2	**Requests by the MIB for further information and referrals to the Secretary of State**	☐
7.3	**Standard letters**	☐
L18	Letter serving the particulars of claim on the defendant (to include the MIB if a defendant)	☐
L19	Letter to the MIB giving notice of service of the particulars of claim	☐
L20	Letter to the MIB giving notice of the filing of a defence	☐
L21	Letter to the MIB serving the amended particulars of claim/documents to be served therewith	☐
L22	Letter to the medical expert warning all reports/letters to be sent by fax	☐

L23	Letter to the MIB providing notice of the trial date being fixed/ notice of filing of the allocation/listing questionnaire, etc	☐
L24	Letter to the court serving the allocation or listing questionnaire	☐
L25	Letter to the Secretary of State to request a decision on the reasonableness of the MIB's request	☐
L26	Letter to the MIB enclosing a copy of the letter to the Secretary of State requesting a decision on the reasonableness of the MIB's further information request	☐
7.4	**Checklist**	☐
CL3	1999 Uninsured Drivers Agreement Notice checklist	☐
7.5	**Diary entries**	☐

7.1 NOTICE REQUIREMENTS

There are multiple notice requirements contained within the 1999 Agreement. For a brief overview refer to the notice checklist.[1] However, please note that it should only be used by reference to the whole of this guide.

7.1.1 Service of the particulars of claim[2]

> Letters L18 and L19

If the particulars of claim are not served with the claim form, notice of service of the particulars of claim must be given to the MIB within seven days of the date of service on the defendant.[3] Ideally, the particulars of claim should be served with the claim form in all cases to avoid the requirement of serving further notice to the MIB. The particulars of claim will also need to be served on the MIB if it has been added as a second defendant.

Once the particulars of claim have been served, a further letter should be sent to the MIB within seven days of service on the defendant.[4] The wording of the Agreement is specific in that it states that the notice is to be given within seven days *of service on the defendant*. Therefore, the notice can only be given once service has been effected on the defendant; the date of effective service is summarised in the table below, but see r 6.7 of the Civil Procedure Rules.

---

1   See 7.4, checklist CL3.
2   The Revised Notes for Guidance 2002, at Clause 5(3), state that if the MIB is added as a defendant, Clause 9(3), which contains the requirement for notice of service of the particulars of claim, need not be complied with. See 2.5.
3   See 7.3, letter L18.
4   See 7.3, letter L19.

Method of service of the particulars of claim	Deemed date of service	Period to give notice to the MIB (from date sent to the defendant)
First class post	The second day after it was posted	2–9 days
Fax	If transmitted on a business day before 4 pm, on that day; if afterwards, the next working day	Depends on time and day of fax
Document exchange	The second day after it was left at the document exchange	2–9 days
Delivering the document to or leaving it at a permitted address	The day after it was delivered to or left at the permitted address	Depends on date of delivery/leaving
Other electronic method	The second day after the day on which it was transmitted	2–9 days

7.1.2 Filing of the defence

7.1.2.1 By the defendant[5]

Letter L20

Notice must be given to the MIB within seven[6] days of the filing of a defence. Therefore, once proceedings have been issued, the file must be reviewed no less than once every three days, until the defence has been filed and notice given. The wording of the Agreement refers to the 'filing' of a defence, not 'receipt' of the defence by the claimant. Therefore, the court should be telephoned at least

---

5   The Revised Notes for Guidance 2002, at Clause 5(3), state that if the MIB is added as a defendant, Clause 11(1)(a) of the Agreement, which contains the requirement for notice of filing of a defence, need not be complied with. See 2.5.

6   The Revised Notes for Guidance 2002, at Clause 7(2), state that notice need only be given to the MIB within 14 days of the proven date of receipt of the document by the claimant. See 2.5.

every seven days to check whether a defence has been filed, with a full attendance note kept of the conversation.[7] Once a defence has been filed, notice must be given to the MIB.[8]

7.1.2.2 *By the MIB*

> ## Letter L20

If the MIB is added as a defendant to the proceedings, the filing of its defence leads to a requirement to give notice to the MIB within seven days of the filing date of that defence. This may seem illogical and unnecessary, but on strict interpretation of the Agreement, it is essential. Use the same procedure as detailed in 7.1.2.1.

7.1.3 Amendment to the particulars of claim/documents required to be served therewith

> ## Letter L21

The MIB must be given notice of any amendments to such documents within seven days.

Documents that fall under this heading will include the following.

7.1.3.1 *The claim form*

For example, where the limitation on the value of the case is changed.

7.1.3.2 *The particulars of claim*

7.1.3.3 *The schedule of special damage and loss*

---

7   If a defence has been filed and the court clerk erroneously assures you that it has not, such an attendance note may not assist your client in getting the MIB to satisfy the judgment, but it will certainly assist you in any subsequent negligence action.

8   See 7.3, letter L20.

7.1.3.4 Medical reports

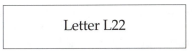

Letter L22

A medical report must be served with the particulars of claim if the claimant intends to rely on it.[9] If a new report is obtained from the same expert, or amendments are made to the report initially served with the particulars of claim, then notice must be given to the MIB within seven days of the new report or amendment being created.[10]

Even if a completely new report is obtained, it is arguable that notice must be given to the MIB within seven days of the creation of it. It is the authors' opinion that this would be too wide an interpretation of the clause; however, this issue has yet to be tested and resolved by the court.

It will be necessary to warn the expert of this time limit and explain that any reports in this case must be faxed on the same date as the report is created, and that the report should be dated with the date of the report, not the date of examination, which would cause problems as the report is often not prepared until some weeks or months after the examination.

7.1.3.5 The notice of funding

Letter L21

As such documents should be created by the claimant's solicitor, this notice should be straightforward.[11]

7.1.3.6 Amendment by another claimant to the proceedings

If there is more than one claimant to the proceedings, filing by the other claimant of any one of the documents referred to in 7.1.3 creates a requirement to give notice to the MIB within seven days of the production of the document; ensure that a copy of the document is served on the MIB.[12]

---

9   CPR, Pt 16, PD para 4.3.

10 Clause 11(1): 'MIB shall incur no liability under MIB's obligation unless the claimant has, not later than seven days after the occurrence of any of the following events, namely: (b) any amendment to the particulars of claim or any amendment of or addition to any schedule or other document required to be served therewith.'

11 See 7.3, letter L21.

12 See 7.3, letter L21.

7.1.3.7   Revised Notes for Guidance 2002

See 2.5. These stipulate that where the MIB is added as a defendant to the proceedings, this notice requirement no longer applies. If the MIB is not added as a defendant to the proceedings, the period for giving notice is extended to 14 days.

7.1.4   Trial date applied for or fixed by the court (seven days)

Letter L23

The claimant must give notice to the MIB within seven days of the trial date being applied for, or the court notifying the claimant of the trial date being fixed.[13] This can occur by one or more of the methods detailed below.

A special MIB reference will ensure any incoming documents are delivered to the fee-earner as a matter of urgency, to allow maximum time to comply with the notice requirement. See 3.1.5.

7.1.4.1   Allocation or listing questionnaire filed by the claimant[14]

Whenever an allocation or listing questionnaire is sent to the court, a letter providing notice to the MIB should be sent within seven days. In practice, this should not be difficult to comply with as a copy is sent to all other solicitors when a copy is sent to the court, if not before. However, it is only by sending the document to the court that the claimant is applying to set the case down for trial.

7.1.4.2   Allocation directions issued by the court including a warned period or fixed date for the trial

Letter L23

Once allocation directions are provided, notice should be sent to the MIB within seven days.

---

13   See 7.3, letter L23.

14   The 1999 Agreement was drafted before the Civil Procedure Rules were finalised. A case was set down by filing a setting down notice, which has now in effect been replaced by the allocation and listing questionnaires. The wording of Clause 11(1)(c) reads as though the notice should be given from the date the court actually sets the matter down for a hearing date, ie, within seven days of a date or period being fixed, not received by the claimant.

7.1.4.3   The court fixes a date for the trial after filing of listing questionnaires

Letter L23

Another interpretation of Clause 11(1)(i) of the Agreement is that the notice must be given to the MIB within seven days of the date a warned period or trial date is actually allocated by the court, rather than the date that the claimant receives the notification of that date. Again, as with the notice for filing of a defence in 7.1.2, the court should be telephoned every three days after filing an allocation or listing questionnaire to see whether a date has been allocated.[15]

7.1.4.4   Revised Notes for Guidance 2002

See 2.5. These stipulate that where the MIB is added as a defendant to the proceedings, this notice requirement no longer applies. If the MIB is not added as a defendant to the proceedings, the period for giving notice is extended to 14 days.

7.1.5   Application for judgment (35 days)

Letter L15

Notice must be given to the MIB at least 35 days before the claimant makes any application for judgment.[16] The Agreement was finalised before the impact of the Woolf reforms, and consequently does not cover the position where the court enters judgment of its own volition. To avoid this scenario occurring, on filing of the allocation questionnaire, a letter should be sent, informing the court that the MIB is involved, and stating that the claimant is not requesting that judgment should be entered. Any application for default or summary judgment should not be sent before the 35 day period has expired. Amendments may have to be made to a case management system to ensure it does not produce requests for default judgment in cases involving the MIB without the required notice being given.

7.1.5.1   Revised Notes for Guidance 2002[17]

These stipulate that where the MIB is added as a defendant to the proceedings, this notice requirement no longer applies. If the MIB is not a defendant to the

---

15   See 7.3, letter L23.
16   See 6.7, letter L15.
17   See 2.5.

proceedings, the Revised Notes provide that the 35 day notice requirement does not apply where the court enters judgment of its own volition.

7.2 REQUESTS BY THE MIB FOR FURTHER INFORMATION AND REFERRALS TO THE SECRETARY OF STATE

> ### Letters L25 and L26

Any request by the MIB for further information or further documentation must be complied with within a reasonable period of time, so long as the request is reasonable. Any questions of reasonableness must be referred to the Secretary of State for Transport (Clause 19). There are no published results of referrals to the Secretary of State and the decisions reached by him. The website **www.mib-help.co.uk** will soon provide details of decisions made by the Secretary of State and provide details of MIB case law.

If the MIB makes a request for information and/or documentation, which those acting on behalf of the claimant consider is not reasonable and wish the matter to be referred to the Secretary of State, notice in writing must be given to both the Secretary of State and the MIB.

The difficulty with this clause[18] is that the request for information will not be flagged to stand out as such. There is no requirement for the MIB to refer to the clause of the Agreement and highlight that it is a request pursuant to that clause, although it would be good practice to do so. Therefore, it will appear as a normal request in standard correspondence for further information, which might often be ignored or overlooked. It must not be. As soon as a request for information of any type is received, it must either be responded to as soon as possible, or a letter must immediately be sent to the Secretary of State asking him to determine whether the request is reasonable.[19] A copy of your request should be sent to the MIB.[20]

---

18 Clause 11(2) of the 1999 Uninsured Drivers Agreement.
19 See 7.3, letter L25.
20 See 7.3, letter L26.

7.3   STANDARD LETTERS

L18   Letter serving the particulars of claim on the defendant (to include the MIB if a defendant)

(1) Defendant at address for service

(2) Motor Insurers' Bureau

[Registered Office]

BY FAX AND RECORDED DELIVERY:

Dear

Claimant:
Defendant:
Accident date:
County court:
Claim no:

We enclose by way of service:

(1) the sealed particulars of claim;

(2) medical reports of *(list all)*;[21]

(3) schedule of loss, damage and expense;

(4) supporting documentation *(list)*;

(5) notice of funding (CFA/CLS);

(6) the response pack.

Please acknowledge receipt by return.

Yours

---

21   See 5.7. The documents at points (2) to (6) should already have been served with the claim
form. This covers the situation if further documents have been obtained since issue.

L19 Letter to the MIB giving notice of service of the particulars of claim

Motor Insurers' Bureau
[Registered Office]

BY FAX AND RECORDED DELIVERY:

Dear

Claimant:
Defendant:
Accident date:
County court:
Claim no:
Date particulars of claim were served by first class post on the defendant:
Date of service:
Date particulars of claim served by fax on the MIB:
Date of service on the MIB:

We confirm that the particulars of claim in this action were served on the date(s) detailed above. We enclose the following:

(1) the sealed particulars of claim;

(2) medical reports of *(list all)*;[22]

(3) schedule of loss, damage and expense;

(4) supporting documentation *(list)*;

(5) notice of funding (CFA/CLS);

(6) the response pack.

This letter constitutes notice under Clause 9(3) of the Motor Insurers' Bureau Uninsured Drivers Agreement 1999.

Please acknowledge receipt by return.

Yours

---

22 See 5.7. The documents at points (2) to (6) should already have been served with the claim form. This covers the situation if further documents have been obtained since issue.

L20 Letter to the MIB giving notice of the filing of a defence

Motor Insurers' Bureau
[Registered Office]

BY FAX AND RECORDED DELIVERY:

Dear

Claimant:
Claim no:
Defendant:
Date defence filed at court:
Party defence filed by (defendant x or the MIB):

We enclose a copy of the defence filed by the above defendant on the date detailed above.

This letter constitutes notice under Clause 11(1)(a) of the Motor Insurers' Bureau Uninsured Drivers Agreement 1999.

Yours

L21   Letter to the MIB serving the amended particulars of claim/documents to be served therewith

Motor Insurers' Bureau
[Registered Office]

BY FAX AND RECORDED DELIVERY:

Dear

Claimant:
Claim no:
Uninsured defendant:
Date of amended particulars of claim:

We confirm an amended particulars of claim/claim form/schedule of special damage and loss/medical report/notice of funding has been filed by (1st/2nd claimant). We attach a copy of that document.

Please acknowledge receipt by return.

Yours

L22   Letter to the medical expert warning all reports/letters to be sent by fax

BY FAX:

Dear

Claimant:
Defendant:
Accident date:
County court:
Claim no:

We are pursuing a claim against the Motor Insurers' Bureau (the MIB) for our above-named client.

One of the requirements of receiving compensation from the MIB is that if a medical report is prepared, a copy must be sent to the MIB within seven days of its production.

Please note that failure by the claimant to send a report within this timescale may result in the claimant receiving no compensation.

In the circumstances, please follow the following instructions:

(1) Any report or communication must be faxed to us on the date of creation.

(2) If the report or communication is dated or completed after an examination of the claimant, please ensure that the document is dated on the date of completion, not the date of examination, and that it is faxed on that same date.

Please acknowledge receipt of this letter.

Yours

L23   Letter to the MIB providing notice of the trial date being fixed/notice of filing of the allocation/listing questionnaire, etc

Motor Insurers' Bureau
[Registered Office]

BY FAX AND RECORDED DELIVERY:

Dear

Claimant:
Claim no:
Uninsured defendant:

We hereby provide you with notice pursuant to Clause 11(1) of the Uninsured Drivers Agreement 1999 that a trial date has been fixed/an application has been made *(delete as appropriate)* for a trial date.

We enclose the *(delete as appropriate)* allocation/listing questionnaire/notice of trial date/notice of allocation, confirming the trial period.

Please acknowledge receipt.

Yours

L24 Letter to the court serving the allocation or listing questionnaire

The Chief Clerk
County court

BY HAND/FAX:

Dear

.... v .... **and Motor Insurers' Bureau**

We enclose the allocation/listing questionnaire with the appropriate fee.

Please note that the Motor Insurers' Bureau (MIB) is involved in proceedings. As notice must be given to it as soon as a warned period or trial date is fixed, please advise by fax as soon as this occurs.

Failure by the claimant to notify the MIB within seven days of a hearing date being fixed may result in the claimant receiving no compensation and also to a potential negligence claim. In the circumstances, we would ask that the notification of a fixing of any date in relation to this case be forwarded on to us on the same date by fax.

Yours

L25   Letter to the Secretary of State to request a decision on the reasonableness of the MIB's request

The Secretary of State for Transport
[Address]

BY FAX AND RECORDED DELIVERY:

Dear

Claimant:
Uninsured defendant:
Accident date:

We refer to the above matter, a claim against an uninsured driver involving the MIB. We request that the Secretary of State make a determination as to the reasonableness of a request by the MIB, pursuant to Clause 19 of the 1999 Uninsured Drivers Agreement.

The request received was as follows:

[Insert details of request]

We object to the request and consider the same to be unreasonable on the following grounds:

[Insert grounds why the request is considered to be unreasonable]

We would invite the Minister to review the following documentation:

[List enclosures]

We await receipt of the Minister's reasoned decision.

Yours

CC: MIB

L26 Letter to the MIB enclosing a copy of the letter to the Secretary of State requesting a decision on the reasonableness of the MIB's further information request

The Motor Insurers' Bureau
[Registered Address]

BY FAX AND RECORDED DELIVERY:

Dear

Claimant:
Uninsured defendant:
Accident date:

We enclose a copy of our referral to the Secretary of State for a determination as to the reasonableness of your recent request.

Please acknowledge receipt.

Yours

7.4 CL3 1999 UNINSURED DRIVERS AGREEMENT NOTICE CHECKLIST

NB: This is a brief summary only, please refer to the relevant paragraphs for full details

Notice requirement	Clause	Notice period (time by which the MIB is to receive notice)	Chapter no	Comment	Multiple notices required?
Pre-issue of proceedings					
Demand insurance details from third party driver	13	ASARP[23]	4.1.2	Demand immediately on receipt of instructions from client	Each time a new driver is identified
Complain to police for failure to supply insurance details	13	ASARP	4.1.6	7 days after request for insurance details	Each time details are demanded from a driver
Lodge MIB application form	7	3 years	2.3.1	Keep a stock of MIB application forms	
Use all reasonable endeavours to obtain name and address of registered keeper of the vehicle (and demand insurance details)	7	ASARP	4.1.3/4		Each time new registered keeper is identified
Service of notices on the MIB only by: • Fax, or • Recorded delivery	8		2.3.2.1	Fax is the safest method as instantaneous	
Post-issue of proceedings					
Notice of issue of proceedings	9(1)	within 14 days of issue	6.5.1		

				Serve with claim form on each occasion[24]	If more than one defendant
If the particulars of claim are served separately, sealed copy with notice to the MIB	9(3)	7 days	7.1.1		(1) Defendant, **including the MIB** if added as a defendant (2) If more than one defendant
Notice of confirmation of service of proceedings:					
• Court confirms service	10(3)(a)(i)	7 days	6.5.2.4	Never allow court to serve proceedings	
• Defendant confirms service	10(3)(a)(ii)	7 days	6.5.2.3	Check file for calls from the defendant every 3 days after proceedings served	
• Personal service	10(3)(a)(iii)	7 days	6.5.2.2		
• Deemed date of service	10(3)(b)	14 days	6.5.2.1		
Notice of filing of a defence at court	11(1)(a)	7 days	7.1.2.1/2	Note wording, 7 days from the **filing** of defence at court, not receipt by the claimant	(1) If more than one defendant (2) Notice to the MIB of the MIB filing a defence if added as a defendant
Notice of amendment to the particulars of claim (or any amendment of or addition to any schedule or other document required to be served therewith)	11(1)(b)	7 days	7.1.3	Beware schedules of special damages, medical report, etc	(1) If more than one defendant (2) If more than one claimant, notices to be provided for each other claimant too

23 As soon as reasonably possible.
24 See footnote 15 at 5.7.

Notice requirement	Clause	Notice period (time by which the MIB is to receive notice)	Chapter no	Comment	Multiple notices required?
Setting down of the case for trial	11(1)(c) (i)	7 days	7.1.4	Consider allocation questionnaire/ listing questionnaire	Likely
Notice to the MIB when notice of trial date is received from the court	11(1)(c) (ii)	7 days	7.1.4	Beware directions order providing trial date/warned period	Likely (warned then fixed date)
Notice of intention to apply for judgment	12	35 days	7.1.5		
Reasonable requests by the MIB for further information	11(2)	A reasonable time	7.2	Disputes as to questions of reasonableness referred to the Secretary of State	Yes, each request

7.5   DIARY ENTRIES

Document reference	Description	Number of days
	General review of file[25]	Every 7 days
	Beware of any request by the MIB's solicitors for further information. Respond as soon as possible or ask the Secretary of State to determine reasonableness of request	Every time correspondence is received from the MIB
L19	Notice of service of the particulars of claim (if separate from claim form)	As soon as service has been effected, but must be done within 7 days
	Check that the MIB has acknowledged receipt of notice of service of the particulars of claim	Every 2 days after letter L19 sent until positive response is received
	Check with the court (by telephone) whether the defence has been filed	Every 3 days after service of particulars of claim has been effected until positive response
L20	Notice to the MIB that the defence has been filed	As soon as the court has confirmed that the defence has been filed; but must be done within 7 days
	Check that the MIB has acknowledged receipt of notice of filing of defence	Every 2 days after letter L20 sent until positive response
L21	If amendments to any documents set out in letter L21, notice of amended document should be sent to the MIB	As soon as document has been so amended, but at least within 7 days
L22	Once proceedings are issued, send L22 to any expert instructed on the file	On issue of proceedings

---

25   See 7.4, checklist CL3.

Document reference	Description	Number of days
L23	Check that listing questionnaires have not been sent, the trial date applied for or trial date fixed; if any such steps have been taken, then give notice to the MIB	Every 7 days
	Check with the court (by telephone) whether a hearing date (or warned period) has been fixed	Every 3 days after the allocation or listing questionnaire is lodged

CHAPTER 8

HEADS OF CLAIM

CHAPTER SUMMARY

8.1	**Parts of the claim that the MIB does not have to satisfy**	☐
8.1.1	Property damage (Clause 16)	☐
8.1.2	Claims made for the benefit of someone other than the claimant (Clause 6(1)(c))	☐
8.1.3	Claims which have been met by other sources of compensation (Clauses 15(b)(ii) and 17)	☐

8.1 PARTS OF THE CLAIM THAT THE MIB DOES NOT HAVE TO SATISFY

The claim made by the claimant should be issued against the uninsured driver, with the usual heads of claim set out in a schedule of special damage. The MIB will either be the second defendant or will have to satisfy the judgment at the conclusion of proceedings. However, due to the operation of Clauses 6(1)(c), 15(2)(b)(ii), 16 and 17, the amount that the MIB will have to pay is likely to be less than the full judgment amount, a point to remember when negotiating.

It is also worth remembering that the shortfall can still be claimed against the uninsured driver. Even if the driver is not insured, there is often no reason why he cannot meet the claim for items such as the policy excess for property damage that the MIB will not have to pay. The precise terms of the assignment and agreement form signed by the claimant before receipt of compensation will have to be amended to allow the claimant to continue to seek damages from the defendant for the items excluded by the MIB.[1]

The heads of claims of which the MIB does not have to pay the full amount are set out below.

---

1   See 11.1.1.

8.1.1 Property damage (Clause 16)

The MIB will not pay the first £300[2] of any claim for property damage and will not pay for any property damage (or losses arising therefrom) in excess of £250,000.[3]

8.1.2 Claims made for the benefit of someone other than the claimant (Clause 6(1)(c))

Any claim which is made for the benefit of another does not have to be satisfied by the MIB. Therefore, any subrogated, assigned or contractual claim will be excluded.

Examples are as follows:

- repairs to the claimant's car paid for by his insurance company;[4]
- earnings to be repaid to the employer in the event of a successful personal injury claim;[5]
- credit hire charges which have yet to be paid;[6]
- private healthcare costs.[7]

However, claims for gratuitous care and assistance provided by friends and relatives, which could be argued to be claims for the benefit of another, will be satisfied by the MIB, at least whilst the Revised Notes for Guidance 2002 remain in force.[8]

---

2   The 'specified excess' referred to in Clause 16 is £300, according to the original Notes for Guidance (and the Revised Notes for Guidance 2002). This means that in the majority of cases, the claimant will not be able to claim their policy excess.

3   This will include the claim for any vehicle damage, personal belongings ruined in the accident, as well as damage to buildings, etc.

4   This would also be excluded under Clause 17(b) – see below.

5   Many claimants recover sick pay during their time off work and there is a term in their contract that these must be repaid in the event of a successful claim for personal injury. The precise contract of employment needs to be checked to see whether the sick payments are effectively merely a loan which has to be repaid (in which case, it is arguable that the MIB would still have to satisfy that claim) or that there is a condition that the claimant must include in any claim a contractual or subrogated claim on behalf of his employer (in which case, the MIB will not have to satisfy such a claim).

6   The law on this area is complex and has constantly evolved over the last couple of years; it is not intended to explore it within the ambit of this publication. Again, the actual hire agreement will have to be studied and if it envisages a subrogated claim, then the MIB will not have to satisfy it.

7   Again, this is also excluded under Clause 17 (see below).

8   This is a concession made by the MIB in Clause 3(4) of the Revised Notes for Guidance 2002: see 2.4.1.

8.1.3 Claims which have been met by other sources of compensation (Clauses 15(b)(ii) and 17)

Benefits or compensation paid to the claimant by any other person for the death, bodily injury or other damage to which the proceedings relate (Clause 15(b)(ii)) and compensation received from the Policyholders Protection Board, any insurer or any other source for death, bodily injury or any other damage to which the proceedings relate (Clause 17) can be reclaimed by the MIB.

In normal personal injury claims, if the claimant had the foresight to take out an insurance policy that paid out in the event of personal injury, the court cannot take into account such payments in assessing the compensation payable to the claimant by the defendant. However, under Clause 15(b)(ii), the claimant will have to repay the MIB any sum paid to him by any other person by way of such compensation or benefits.

Examples are as follows:

- payments made under a personal accident, long term disability or critical illness scheme (whether by way of a lump sum or instalments);[9]
- payments made to compensate the claimant for loss of earnings by an insurance policy;
- payments made pursuant to the claimant's household insurance policy in respect of items damaged in the vehicle.

This includes a continuing obligation to repay the MIB for any subsequent payments made after the judgment is entered.[10]

However, some payments made to the claimant as a result of the accident should not be deductible – if, for instance, the claimant had a policy whereby his mortgage was repaid by an insurer in the event of an accident, such payment(s) should not be deducted as they are not compensation for death or bodily injury or other damage to which the proceedings relate.

---

9   This is important to take into account when negotiating, as such payments may sometimes effectively wipe out general damage awards and even some loss of earnings claims.

10 Clause 15(b); however, the MIB cannot compel a claimant to claim under a different policy.

CHAPTER 9

SETTLEMENT AND COSTS

CHAPTER SUMMARY

9.1   SETTLEMENT OF THE CLAIM

Although the MIB is only bound under the terms of the 1999 Agreement to satisfy a claim where judgment is obtained, in practical terms, it is keen to negotiate a settlement and settle the claim when possible to do so.

The MIB will negotiate 'in the shoes of the defendant' and settle a claim prior to issue of proceedings where possible.

9.1.1   Assignment and agreement forms

Letter L27

The MIB will need an assignment and agreement form completed, which assigns all rights of the claimant to the MIB to pursue a claim against the uninsured driver. The assignment and agreement form does not allow the claimant to pursue the defendant for any claim not paid for by the MIB (for example, a subrogated claim for the £300 excess). Therefore, the claimant must be advised on the terms of the form and be warned that he is assigning his rights over to the MIB.[1]

9.2 COSTS

9.2.1 Conditional fee agreements and success fees

9.2.1.1 *Insurance policy premiums*

It is understood that the MIB will pay for after the event legal expense insurance policies and has been ordered to do so.[2]

9.2.1.2 *Success fees*

The MIB has also indicated that it might argue that the success fee is a subrogated claim by the solicitor. Again, using the reasoning below, this claim by the MIB should not be successful. Indeed, courts have already ordered the MIB to pay the success fee of a solicitor.[3]

9.2.2 Before the event legal expense insurance

It has been indicated that the MIB may argue that if before the event legal expense insurance is in place, that is, a pre-existing policy of insurance under which the claimant could make a claim, the MIB should be able to avoid the payment of costs as a subrogated claim pursuant to Clause 6(1)(c)(ii).

The authors believe that the MIB will not be successful on this point for the following reasons:

(1) Clause 17 of the 1999 Agreement only allows the MIB to set-off payments which have already been received by the claimant by way of compensation under the terms of an insurance agreement or arrangement, the Policyholders Protection Board or any other source.

When the claimant makes his claim against the MIB, he will not have received payment for his legal costs under the terms of the before the event legal expense insurance policy, and in any event, payment of costs would not amount to 'compensation'. Therefore, the MIB cannot invoke this clause to support the contention that it should not pay costs.

(2) Whilst Clause 15(b)(ii) obliges the claimant to repay any compensation or benefit which he receives after judgment which would have been

---

1   See 9.3, letter L27.
2   *Lunt v Conran* (2001) unreported, 19 December, Oldham county court.
3   See *Lunt v Conran* above.

deductible under Clause 17 had it been received earlier, this would not cover the position where there is legal expense insurance in force. In a case where the MIB is ordered to pay the claimant's costs, the claimant will never receive any payment with regard to his costs from the legal expense insurer.

Clause 6 of the 1999 Agreement only provides the MIB with the right to avoid payment for a claim on behalf of another. The costs are not part of 'the claim', they are a separate issue and the claim for costs is for the claimant, not on behalf of another.

However, this issue remains untested, as does the issue of whether a legal expense insurance policy should be disclosed under Clause 9 as part of the 'Proper Notice'[4] bundle. At this time, it will probably be wise to disclose such a policy as there is no disadvantage to the claimant of doing so, whilst if the court held that non-disclosure breached Clause 9(2), the consequences could be fatal to the claim.

The Motor Accident Solicitors Society (MASS)[5] and the authors through their developing website[6] intend to maintain a list of MIB cases dealing with all key points.

---

4   See 5.4.

5   See Appendix F.

6   www.mib-help.co.uk.

9.3   STANDARD LETTERS

L27   Letter to the client enclosing the MIB assignment and agreement form

Client address

Dear

Claim against:
Incident date:

I enclose a form of assignment and agreement received from the Motor Insurers' Bureau (MIB). Before it forwards the agreed compensation in this claim to you, this form must be signed and returned to the MIB. You are not entitled to receive any money from the MIB unless you complete the form.

The form confirms that if the MIB, who is settling your claim, decides to pursue a claim against the uninsured driver (to attempt to recover the monies it has paid to you), you must assist it with that claim, but you would not be at risk if any costs order is made against you if the claim pursued was unsuccessful. It is standard practice to complete this form in claims against the MIB, to allow the MIB to attempt to recover the monies it paid to you from the uninsured driver if it believes that there are realistic prospects of doing so. In most cases, it takes no further action.

You will appreciate that as your claim has been settled under the terms of the 1999 Uninsured Drivers Agreement, there was a £300 excess which we have not received. By completing the form of assignment and agreement, you lose the right to attempt to recover those sums yourself, as you are assigning your right to claim to the MIB.

Please read the form through and sign and date it on the last page where indicated. If you have any questions, please do not hesitate to telephone me.

Yours

CHAPTER 10

APPORTIONMENT OF DAMAGES

CHAPTER SUMMARY

10.1   Accounting to the claimant   ☐

10.1   ACCOUNTING TO THE CLAIMANT

Clause 21 deals with the situation where the claimant obtains judgment which is not satisfied by the defendant, which includes liabilities other than relevant liabilities that the MIB must satisfy. When the MIB compensates the claimant, it insists that the applicant assigns his rights to the MIB. In the (admittedly rare) event of the MIB successfully obtaining full or partial satisfaction of the assigned claim, it must account to the claimant for the amount received for liabilities other than the relevant liabilities (which it has already paid to the claimant). In the event of partial satisfaction, an apportionment is to be made.

In practice, this situation rarely if ever arises, as the uninsured defendant is unlikely to have the means to satisfy any judgment and the MIB is therefore unlikely to waste the costs of pursuing him.

CHAPTER 11

RECOVERY SECTION – MIB CLAIMS GOING WRONG

CHAPTER SUMMARY

11.1   INSURER OR THE MIB

> Letters L28 and L29

Circumstances can arise where an insurer denies that it should indemnify the defendant, whilst the MIB will submit that the insurer should deal with the claim. For example, the insurer claims that the driver of the insured vehicle is not identified, therefore, it does not have to deal with the claim as a Road Traffic Act insurer pursuant to s 151 of the Road Traffic Act 1988, as judgment cannot be obtained against 'any person'.[1] Instead, it argues that it is an MIB untraced claim (see 4.1.1).[2]

Guidance was given in 1.2 as to which organisation should deal with the claim. Once it is decided which organisation should deal with it, ensure

---

1   Section 151(2)(b) of the Road Traffic Act 1988.
2   This argument is common and highlights the need for early identification of the driver.

unequivocal confirmation is obtained from them (see letters L28 and L29).[3] Without such written confirmation, there is a risk that if the court decides (for instance) that the insurer will not have to indemnify the defendant, proper notices will not have been provided to the MIB because the claim was not being dealt with as an MIB claim. Therefore, the MIB will also be able to avoid satisfying the judgment.

Where there is any doubt, proceed on the basis of providing notice to the insurer (before or within seven days of proceedings) of the bringing of proceedings,[4] and the notices to the MIB under the terms of the 1999 Agreement.

11.1.1 Domestic Regulation Insurer (now Article 75 of the Memorandum and Articles of Association)

If an insurer advises that it is dealing as a 'Domestic Regulation Insurer', or under the terms of 'Article 75', it is in effect acting in the shoes of the MIB, and all terms of the 1999 Agreement will have to be complied with. Notice must be given in these circumstances in accordance with the terms of the 1999 Agreement, and for the sake of certainty should be given to the MIB and the insurer, with the additional notice to the insurer (before or within seven days of proceedings) of the bringing of proceedings,[5] until you have unequivocal confirmation in writing that notice need only be given to one or the other.

11.2 CORRECT NOTICE NOT GIVEN TO THE MIB

> Letter L30

If notice has not been given in accordance with the Agreement, or the MIB alleges that correct notice has not been provided, unless the MIB confirms unequivocally that it will not raise the issue of the (alleged) incorrect notice at any stage of the proceedings,[6] the only alternative is to discontinue proceedings and reissue them against the defendant, providing the correct notices to the MIB.

---

3   See 11.4.
4   Section 152(1)(a) of the Road Traffic Act 1988.
5   Section 152(1)(a) of the Road Traffic Act 1988.
6   See 11.4, letter L30.

If the MIB states that it 'reserves its position' in respect of the incorrect notice, it can wait for the primary limitation period to expire and then take the notice point, knowing the claimant's claim will then be statute barred.

11.3   UNINSURED OR UNTRACED

A difficulty can arise where the claimant has been given a name by the driver at the scene of the accident, but a driver by that name cannot be located or contacted.[7] The name could either be correct and the driver insured or uninsured (in which case, proceedings could be issued and an order for service by an alternative means[8] obtained for service on the insurer or the MIB), or the name could be false and therefore the claim should be dealt with under the Untraced Drivers Agreement. In that event, it is important that the solicitor acts expeditiously so that the MIB (or the court) makes a decision before the three year limitation period (for either issuing a claim if insured or uninsured, or for lodging an Untraced Drivers Agreement application form)[9] expires.

In cases where the limitation date is looming, proceedings may have to be issued and a claim made under the Untraced Drivers Agreement, although this may have costs implications.

---

7   See 4.1.1 regarding confirming the identity of the driver.
8   See 6.3.1.
9   Clause 1(1)(f) of the Untraced Drivers Agreement 1996.

11.4   STANDARD LETTERS

L28   Letter to the MIB requesting confirmation that it has no interest in the case

Motor Insurers' Bureau
[Registered Office]

BY FAX AND RECORDED DELIVERY:

Dear

Claimant:
Defendant/uninsured driver:
Claim no:

We are now preparing to issue proceedings.

Please confirm in writing by return that *(insert insurance company name)* is a Road Traffic Act insurer for the purpose of our client's claim.

Please also confirm that on issue of proceedings, no notice of issue of proceedings or any other notices are required to be given to the Motor Insurers' Bureau (MIB) pursuant to the 1999 Uninsured Drivers Agreement. Until such written confirmation is received from the MIB and the insurer, we will have no alternative but to correspond with both parties, and provide notice of issue to both parties, thereby increasing the costs in this matter.

We await your confirmation by return.

Yours

L29 Letter to the insurer requesting confirmation that it is dealing with the claim as a Road Traffic Act insurer

Insurer details

BY FAX:

Dear

Our client:
Accident date:
Third party:

We are instructed by the above-named to pursue a claim for damages for personal injuries, losses and expenses incurred as a result of the above accident.

We have been advised by the Motor Insurers' Bureau that you are the Road Traffic Act insurer for the above party.

Please confirm in writing that you are dealing with this claim as a result of your obligations as a Road Traffic Act insurer pursuant to s 151 of the Road Traffic Act 1988. Please also forward full details of the terms of the policy pursuant to s 154 of the Road Traffic Act 1988 to include the following:

(a) The vehicle registration numbers covered by the policy of insurance.

(b) The policy number.

(c) The name of the insured.

(d) The period of the insurance cover.

Until such written confirmation is received from your company and the MIB, we will have no alternative but to correspond with both parties, and provide notice of issue to both parties, thereby increasing the costs in this matter.

Yours

L30 Letter to the MIB confirming it will not take issue on provision of an incorrect notice

Motor Insurers' Bureau
[Registered Office]

BY FAX AND RECORDED DELIVERY:

Dear

Claimant:
Defendant/uninsured driver:
Claim no:

We refer to your letter in which you state that we have failed to give correct notice pursuant to *(insert relevant clause number)* of the 1999 Uninsured Drivers Agreement.

Whilst we do not accept that notice has not been properly provided, unless you confirm unequivocally by return that at no time in the future will you ask the court or the Secretary of State to determine whether correct notice was provided on this occasion and/or submit that the MIB should not have to satisfy any judgment due to any such alleged breach of the terms of the 1999 Agreement, we will have no alternative but to discontinue proceedings and commence new proceedings against the uninsured driver, thereby increasing the costs of this claim.

For the avoidance of doubt, we set out below the terms of the notice with which you state we have failed to comply:

Clause number of the Agreement	
Clause requirement	
Date of our letter to you providing notice	
Enclosures *(list)*	
Date of your letter stating notice provisions not complied with	

We await your response by return.

Yours

CHAPTER 12

THE 1988 UNINSURED DRIVERS AGREEMENT

CHAPTER SUMMARY

This chapter summarises the Motor Insurers' Bureau (Compensation of Victims of Uninsured Drivers) Agreement 1988 ('the 1988 Agreement'), highlighting the main differences between that and the 1999 Agreement. Reference is made to the earlier chapters in relation to the 1999 Agreement where the law remains the same.[1]

12.1	**Application of the 1988 Agreement**	☐
12.2	**The basic Agreement**	☐
12.3	**Conditions precedent (Clause 5(1))**	☐
12.3.1	Notice in writing of the bringing of proceedings (Clause 5(1)(a))	☐
12.3.2	Provision of information that the MIB may reasonably require (Clause 5(1)(b)(i))	☐
12.3.3	Provision of information regarding insurance cover for property damage (Clause 5(1)(b)(ii))	☐
12.3.4	Demand for information under s 151 of the Road Traffic Act 1972	☐
12.3.5	Notice of intention to apply for judgment	☐
12.4	**Exceptions and limitations**	☐
12.4.1	Excluded vehicles (Clause 6(1)(a), (b))	☐
12.4.2	Use of vehicles not required to be covered by contracts of insurance (Clause 6(1)(b))	☐
12.4.3	Claims for the benefit of another – subrogated claims (Clause 6(1)(c))	☐
12.4.4	Claims where compensation is received from another source (Clause 2(3))	☐
12.4.5	Property damage to a vehicle which was uninsured and the claimant knew it was uninsured (Clause 6(1)(d))	☐

---

1 As the 1988 Agreement only applies to accidents up to and including 30 September 1999, this chapter is brief. The date of publication of this book is after 30 September 2002; therefore, proceedings should have been issued, limitation having expired.

12.4.6 'The passenger exceptions' (Clause 6(1)(e))	☐
12.4.6.1 The burden and standard of proof of such knowledge	☐
12.4.7 Property damage	☐
12.5 Settlement of the claim, costs and assignment and agreement	☐
12.6 Standard letters	☐
L31 Letter to the client to forward to the other driver	☐
L32 Letter from the solicitor requesting insurance details	☐
L33 Letter to the MIB providing notice of intention to apply for judgment	☐

12.1   APPLICATION OF THE 1988 AGREEMENT

The 1988 Agreement relates to accidents which occurred on or after 31 December 1988 and before 1 October 1999.

12.2   THE BASIC AGREEMENT

As with the 1999 Agreement, the MIB is obliged to satisfy outstanding judgments[2] in cases where legislation requires that the relevant liability be insured against by the user of the vehicle (see 2.4.4 for vehicles not required to be covered by contracts of insurance). The obligation only arises where the claimant has complied with various conditions (although these are less onerous than those set out in the 1999 Agreement) (see 12.3) and is limited or absent in certain circumstances (see 12.4).

12.3   CONDITIONS PRECEDENT (CLAUSE 5(1))

12.3.1   Notice in writing of the bringing of proceedings (Clause 5(1)(a))

The MIB will incur no liability to satisfy the judgment unless notice in writing of the bringing of proceedings is given, within seven days after the

---

2   Clause 2(1) of the 1988 Agreement provides that the MIB's obligation is to satisfy a judgment which is not satisfied in full within seven days of the date of judgment being entered.

commencement of proceedings, to the MIB (if the vehicle was not insured or the insurer is not identifiable) or to the insurer (in cases where the vehicle was covered by insurance). Such notice has to be accompanied by a copy of the writ, summons or other document initiating the proceedings.[3] Whilst the 1999 Agreement allows 14 days for such service to take place, the 1988 Agreement allows only seven days – one of the few examples where the 1988 Agreement is more onerous than the 1999 Agreement.

The claimant *must* give proper notice of the bringing of the relevant proceedings not later than seven days from the commencement of proceedings. It does not matter whether or not the MIB is aware of the intention to bring proceedings; it must be given notice that proceedings have been issued. The time limit runs from the date proceedings are in fact issued by the court, NOT from when the claimant (or his solicitor) becomes aware that they have been issued.[4] If notice is given outside the notice period, the MIB does not have to bring it to the attention of the court or the claimant's solicitors until after limitation has expired and can then rely on this point to avoid satisfying the judgment.[5] Therefore, if the requisite notice has not been given, unless the MIB will provide written unequivocal confirmation that the breach will not be relied upon at a later date, the solicitor should discontinue and reissue proceedings prior to limitation expiring.

The notice of issue must include notice in writing that proceedings have been commenced by claim form or writ (the notice of issue), and a copy of the sealed claim form or writ.[6] For guidance on the procedure to be followed, see 6.2. Remember, under the terms of the 1988 Agreement, notice in writing must be received by the MIB within seven days, not 14 days as provided for under the 1999 Agreement.

---

3   The summons/writ have now been replaced by the claim form.

4   See for instance *Silverton v Goodall* [1997] PIQR 451, where the claimant's solicitors did not give the MIB the requisite notice of issue within the relevant time period and served it late because the court did not send the notice to the claimant's solicitors until after that time period had expired (due to unexplained delays in the court office). The claimant's solicitors subsequently joined the MIB as a defendant, and that claim was struck out due to their failure to comply with the notice period. The Court of Appeal upheld that decision.

5   See for instance *Wake v Wylie* [2001] RTR 20; [2001] PIQR 13, a case concerning incorrect notice given to s 151 insurers where the claimant's solicitors were held not to have given proper notice of the bringing of proceedings; the Court of Appeal held that there had been no representation on the insurers' part that might found a claim based on estoppel; it was open to the insurers to wait until judgment had been entered against the driver and recovery then sought from them before arguing that the notice provisions had not been complied with, and therefore the point had not been waived. The same arguments would seem to apply if the case had concerned the MIB.

6   See for instance *Cambridge v Callaghan* (1997) The Times, 21 March, where the Court of Appeal held that the MIB did not have to satisfy a judgment where a copy of an unstamped writ or notice of issue was served.

12.3.2 Provision of information that the MIB may reasonably require (Clause 5(1)(b)(i))

The claimant must furnish the MIB with such information as the MIB may reasonably require. Any question as to the reasonableness of the request will be dealt with by the Secretary of State[7] (see 7.2).

12.3.3 Provision of information regarding insurance cover for property damage (Clause 5(1)(b)(ii))

Clause 5(1)(b)(ii) specifically states that information required by the MIB in relation to any insurance covering damage to property to which the claim relates and any claims made under that insurance should be given to the MIB, although, unlike in the 1999 Agreement, the onus is on the MIB to request the information rather than the claimant to provide it in any event. There are no specific time limits imposed for the provision of such information as the MIB requires.

12.3.4 Demand for information under s 151 of the Road Traffic Act 1972

> Letters L31 and L32

The claimant must have demanded the insurance details of the driver concerned. Again, unlike in the 1999 Agreement, there is no time limit imposed and as long as such a demand has been made prior to the issue of proceedings, the MIB will not be able to evade liability for satisfying the judgment. However, the demand will have to be made and letters should be sent from both the driver and the claimant's solicitor requesting such information.[8] The 1972 Act has now been replaced by the Road Traffic Act 1988 and checks should be made to ensure that the demand is made in accordance with the correct Act (depending on the date).[9]

---

7   Clause 5(2) of the 1988 Agreement.
8   See 12.6, letters L31 and L32.
9   See footnote 1 above.

12.3.5 Notice of intention to apply for judgment

Letter L33

Although not expressly provided for within the terms of the 1988 Agreement, the practice developed that the MIB should be given notice of the intention to apply for judgment 21 days before an application for judgment was made.[10]

12.4 EXCEPTIONS AND LIMITATIONS

12.4.1 Excluded vehicles (Clause 6(1)(a), (b))

Checklist CL1

The MIB excludes claims where the vehicle is a Crown vehicle unless the vehicle is insured. Other vehicles are also excluded from claims against the MIB and are summarised in the checklist at 2.7.

12.4.2 Use of vehicles not required to be covered by contracts of insurance (Clause 6(1)(b))

This exempts the MIB from having to satisfy judgments when the claim arises out of the use of a vehicle which is not required to be covered by insurance – the 'off-road' exception. Prior to 3 April 2000, vehicles only required insurance when they were being used on a public road and, therefore, accidents off public roads would not lead to any liability on the MIB to satisfy the judgment.[11]

12.4.3 Claims for the benefit of another – subrogated claims (Clause 6(1)(c))

Subrogated claims, that is, claims which are made on behalf of another, such as the claimant's insurance company in relation to the repairs to the claimant's car paid for under the terms of his comprehensive insurance, or repayment of sick

---

10 See 12.6, letter L33.
11 See for instance *Clarke v Kato* [1998] 1 WLR 1647; [1998] 4 All ER 417; [1998] PIQR 1, in which the House of Lords held that the MIB did not have to satisfy two judgments obtained against uninsured drivers who had negligently injured innocent third parties who were in a multi-storey car park and on the kerb of a car park, neither place being defined as a 'road'.

pay paid by an employer, will not be recoverable from the MIB. See 8.1.2 for other examples of claims that would be excluded under this clause.

12.4.4 Claims where compensation is received from another source (Clause 2(3))

Benefits or compensation paid to the claimant by any other person, an insurer or any other source, for the death, bodily injury or other damage to which the proceedings relate, and compensation received from the Policyholders Protection Board, can be reclaimed by the MIB.

In normal personal injury claims, if the claimant had the foresight to take out an insurance policy that paid out in the event of personal injury, the court cannot take into account such payments in assessing the compensation payable to the claimant by the defendant. However, under Clause 2(3), the claimant will have to repay the MIB any sum paid to him by any other person by way of such compensation or benefits.

12.4.5 Property damage to a vehicle which was uninsured and the claimant knew it was uninsured (Clause 6(1)(d))

Where the claim is for property damage arising out of the damage to a motor vehicle or the losses arising therefrom, and the claimant knew or ought to have known that the motor vehicle to which the claim relates was uninsured, then the MIB will not have to satisfy any judgment.

12.4.6 'The passenger exceptions' (Clause 6(1)(e))

The MIB will incur no liability to satisfy any part of the judgment in the event that the claimant knew or ought to have known that the vehicle in which he was travelling was either uninsured or had been stolen.[12] The term *'knew or ought to have known'* must be interpreted restrictively[13] and if an ordinary prudent passenger, with the same facts and knowledge available to him as were available to the claimant, would have made enquiries of the existence of insurance for the vehicle, the claimant's carelessness or negligence is not sufficient to allow the MIB to avoid the claim under this permitted exception.

---

12 See also 2.4.2.3.

13 See *White v White and Another* [2001] UKHL 9; [2001] 1 WLR 481; [2001] 2 All ER 43; [2001] PIQR 20, in which the House of Lords held that unless the claimant had actual knowledge that the driver was not insured or had information from which he had drawn the conclusion that the driver might not be insured but had deliberately refrained from asking, lest his suspicions should be confirmed, then the claimant had not 'known or ought to have known'. The claimant who was careless or negligent could not be held to have 'known or ought to have known'.

12.4.6.1   The burden and standard of proof of such knowledge

Under the 1988 Agreement (and the 1972 Agreement), the MIB has to prove on the balance of probabilities that the passenger knew or ought to have known that the driver was uninsured.[14]

12.4.7   Property damage

Under the 1988 Agreement, the first £175 of property damage is not payable, and there is a limit of £250,000 is respect of property damage.

12.5   SETTLEMENT OF THE CLAIM, COSTS AND ASSIGNMENT AND AGREEMENT

See Chapters 9 and 10 dealing with these issues in respect of the 1999 Agreement.

---

14 See *Porter v MIB* [1978] RTR 503, where the claimant owned a vehicle which she requested the defendant to drive. The defendant was uninsured. It was held that as she had no reason to suspect that he was uninsured, and as she had seen him driving at work, the MIB had failed to prove that she knew or ought to have known and had to satisfy the judgment.

12.6   STANDARD LETTERS

L31   Letter to the client to forward to the other driver

This must be sent in all circumstances, other than if the client has already sent and provided a copy of such a letter.

Dear

Road traffic accident date:
Location:

You were involved in a road traffic accident with me on the above date.

I formally demand that you supply to me by return post confirmation that you were insured at the time of the accident, or confirmation that you would have been insured if your insurer had not avoided or cancelled your policy.

Please supply full details of your insurance policy, including the following:

(a) Name of insurer.

(b) Address of insurer.

(c) Policy number.

(d) Date of issue of policy.

(e) Date of expiry of policy.

Please also supply a copy of the insurance policy.

If you were not insured at the time of the accident, please confirm this in writing to me.

Failure to supply this information is an offence under s 154 of the Road Traffic Act 1988 and may result in prosecution by the police.

Please could you also confirm whether or not you are the registered keeper of the vehicle; if not, please supply the name and details of the person who is.

Yours

L32   Letter from the solicitor requesting insurance details

Dear

Our client:
Road traffic accident date:
Location:

You were involved in a road traffic accident with our client on the above date.

We formally demand that you supply to us by return post confirmation that you were insured at the time of the accident, or confirmation that you would have been insured if your insurer had not avoided or cancelled your policy.

Please supply full details of your insurance policy, including the following:

(a) Name of insurer.

(b) Address of insurer.

(c) Policy number.

(d) Date of issue of policy.

(e) Date of expiry of policy.

Please also supply a copy of the insurance policy.

If you were not insured at the time of the accident, please confirm this in writing.

Failure to supply this information is an offence under s 154 of the Road Traffic Act 1988 and may result in prosecution by the police.

Please could you also confirm whether or not you are the registered keeper of the vehicle; if not, please supply the name and details of the person who is.

Yours

L33 Letter to the MIB providing notice of intention to apply for judgment

Motor Insurers' Bureau
[Registered Office]

BY FAX AND RECORDED DELIVERY:

Dear

Claimant:
Defendant/uninsured driver:
County court:
Claim no:

We give you notice that on or after 21 days from today's date, we will apply to the court for judgment.

Please acknowledge receipt by return.

Yours

CHAPTER 13

THE UNTRACED DRIVERS AGREEMENT 1996

CHAPTER SUMMARY

13.1   THE BASIC AGREEMENT

The Untraced Drivers Agreement 1996 provides a non-litigious method to compensate the victims of untraced drivers for injuries, losses and expenses but not property damage.[1] Proceedings cannot be issued by the claimant as there is no known defendant.

13.2   THE DATE IN FORCE (CLAUSE 1(1)(A))

The current Untraced Drivers Agreement came into force in relation to accidents which occurred on or after 1 July 1996. A new Untraced Drivers Agreement is awaiting approval by the government but has not yet been released.

The MIB is obliged to compensate victims of injuries and consequential losses when the applicant is unable to trace the person responsible for the death, injury and loss or, if there is more than one person responsible, is unable to trace one of those persons.[2]

Compensate will be paid if, on the balance of probabilities, the untraced person would be liable to pay damages to the applicant in respect of the death or injury.[3]

The liability concerned must be one that would be required to be covered by insurance pursuant to Part VI of the Road Traffic Act 1988. Therefore, if the applicant would recover damages if the untraced person was located and insured, the MIB will make an award to the applicant.[4]

---

1   The draft Fifth Insurance Directive provides for payment of property damage in cases where the applicant has suffered significant personal injury.
2   See Clause 1(1)(b) of the Agreement.
3   See Clause 1(1)(c) of the Agreement.
4   See Clause 1(1)(d) of the Agreement and 2.4.3, 2.7, checklist CL1.

13.3 CONDITIONS PRECEDENT

13.3.1 The application form (Clause 1(1)(f))

The application form[5] must be fully completed and provided to the MIB within three years from the date of the accident, otherwise the MIB will not accept a claim under the Untraced Drivers Agreement.

13.3.2 Reporting to the police (Clause 1(1)(g))

The incident must be reported to the police within 14 days of the accident or as soon as the applicant reasonably could report the matter. The applicant must co-operate fully with the police.[6]

13.4 EXCEPTIONS AND LIMITATIONS

13.4.1 Children and persons not of full capacity (Clause 2(2))

This clause states that where any act is done to or by a solicitor or other person acting on behalf of the applicant, and any decision is made by or in respect of a solicitor or any person or persons acting on behalf of the applicant, or any sum is paid to a solicitor or any other person acting on behalf of an applicant, then, whatever the age or circumstances of the applicant, that act, etc, shall be treated as if done to an applicant of full age and capacity. Therefore, applications must be made within three years of the accident date if possible.[7]

Where there is any doubt as to the identity of a defendant, an Untraced Drivers Agreement application form must be lodged with the MIB within three years, regardless of the capacity of the applicant. If the claim is pursued under the Uninsured Drivers Agreement and the court decides that the defendant is untraced (for example, where a false name has been given), the claimant will be unable to make a claim pursuant to the Untraced Drivers Agreement if the three years have expired.[8]

---

5   The application form should be obtained from the MIB: see 1.6.2. Such forms may be updated from time to time so ensure that any form used has been recently obtained.

6   See Clause 1(1)(g).

7   See 2.4.1.

8   If there is any doubt about the identity of a defendant, an Untraced Drivers Agreement application form should be lodged before the three year period expires.

13.4.2 Exclusions by knowledge: 'the passenger exceptions' (Clause 1(2))

The 1996 Agreement prevents recovery from the MIB by applicants if they knew that the driver was uninsured,[9] or that the vehicle had been stolen or unlawfully taken,[10] or that the vehicle was being used in the course of or in furtherance of a crime,[11] or the vehicle was being used as a means of escape or avoidance of lawful apprehension.[12]

13.4.2.1 *Knowledge that the driver was uninsured*

The 1996 Agreement allows the MIB to avoid satisfying a judgment where the applicant knew or had reason to believe that there was no policy of insurance in force for the vehicle in which he was travelling. It is likely that the term 'knew or had reason to believe' will be interpreted as restrictively[13] as it has been pursuant to the Uninsured Drivers Agreement 1999, where the House of Lords has held that unless the claimant had actual knowledge that the driver was not insured or had information from which he had drawn the conclusion that the driver might not be insured but had deliberately refrained from asking, lest his suspicions should be confirmed, then the claimant had not 'known or ought to have known' for the purpose of the similar clause in the Uninsured Drivers Agreement 1999. The claimant who was careless or negligent could not be held to have 'known or ought to have known'.

In reality, this exclusion is rarely relevant. If a passenger is unaware of the identity of the defendant, he is unlikely to be aware of his uninsured status.

13.4.2.2 *Knowledge that the vehicle was stolen*

Under the 1996 Agreement, no liability will be incurred by the MIB where the passenger 'knew or had reason to believe'[14] that the vehicle had been stolen or unlawfully taken when he entered the vehicle or after he got in but when he had a reasonable opportunity to get out.

---

9   See Clause 1(2)(b)(ii).
10 See Clause 1(2)(b)(i).
11 See Clause 1(1)(b)(iii).
12 See Clause 1(2)(b)(iv).
13 *White v White and Another* [2001] UKHL 9; [2001] 1 WLR 481; [2001] 2 All ER 43; [2001] PIQR 20.
14 See footnote 13.

13.4.2.3 Knowledge that the vehicle was being used in the course of or in furtherance of a crime

Under the 1996 Agreement, two specific exclusions are introduced where the passenger 'knew or had reason to believe'[15] that the vehicle was being used in the course or furtherance of a crime, or that it was being used as a means of escape from, or avoidance of, lawful apprehension. This could include the following circumstances: driving under the influence of drink or drugs, dangerous driving/driving without due care and attention and other criminal activity.[16]

13.4.2.4 Knowledge that the vehicle was being used as a means of escape from or avoidance of lawful apprehension

Under the 1996 Agreement, no liability would be incurred by the MIB where the passenger 'knew or had reason to believe'[17] that the vehicle was being used as a means of escape, or avoidance of lawful apprehension when he entered the vehicle or after he got in but when he had a reasonable opportunity to get out.

13.4.3 Excluded vehicles

13.4.3.1 Crown vehicles (Clause 1(2)/1(3))

The MIB excludes claims where the vehicle is a Crown vehicle unless the vehicle is insured. Any vehicle unlawfully removed from the possession of the Crown is deemed to be still in the possession of the Crown while it is removed. Therefore, the Crown would have to compensate the victim of any injury caused by the vehicle while it was removed from the Crown's possession.[18]

13.4.3.2 Vehicles used as a weapon (Clause 1(1)(e))

Any vehicle used by the untraced person as a weapon, in a deliberate attempt to cause death or injury of the applicant, is excluded under the 1996 Agreement. Instead, an application should be submitted to the Criminal Injuries Compensation Authority.[19]

---

15 See footnote 13.
16 See 2.4.2.4.
17 See footnote 13.
18 Clause 1(3)(a).
19 See 1.4.

13.4.4 Limitations

13.4.4.1   Property damage (Clause 1(1))

The MIB makes no awards for property damage under the terms of the Agreement.[20]

13.4.4.2   Claims on behalf of an employer (Clause 4)

The MIB will not make payments to employers for salary paid whilst the applicant was injured due to the untraced driver, even where the applicant's contract of employment provides for reimbursement.[21]

13.5   TWO POTENTIAL TORTFEASORS (CLAUSE 5)

If there are two potential tortfeasors, an untraced driver and an identified insured driver, the MIB may request that proceedings be commenced against the identified driver. Due to the principle of joint and several liability, as long as that identified driver is found to have been negligent and that negligence has at least partially caused the accident, the claimant will recover in full against the defendant, and therefore the claim under the Untraced Drivers Agreement need not be proceeded with. This puts the claimant in a more advantageous position (as he can recover property damage and full costs, etc).

If there are two potential tortfeasors, a claim should first be made against the insured driver, but the solicitor should ensure that the issue of liability is determined within three years of the accident regardless of the capacity of the claimant,[22] in order that if the identified driver is found not to have been negligent, a claim under the Untraced Drivers Agreement can be made. In practice, if there is any possibility of the issue of liability being determined after three years from the date of the accident, an Untraced Drivers Agreement application form must be lodged with the MIB.[23]

13.5.1   Judgment obtained against an identified person

Where a judgment is obtained against an identified driver, the MIB will not pay the portion of the award attributable to the untraced driver until the judgment

---

20 Clause 3 provides for payment in respect of death or bodily injury assessed in a like manner as a court would assess damages had the applicant brought successful proceedings against a defendant. Therefore, consequential losses (care, loss of earnings, etc) will be awarded, but see 13.4.4.2.

21 Clause 4 of the 1996 Agreement.

22 See 13.4.1.

23 See 14.1.2.

has not been satisfied fully within three months. Only after three months have elapsed will they pay the portion attributable to the untraced driver. This will only apply if the identified person is uninsured, as otherwise the judgment will usually be satisfied in full by the insurance company.

The table below sets out the circumstances in which an award will be made, the apportionment that will be paid by the MIB, and the time the payment will be made.[24]

Circumstances of payment under the Untraced Drivers Agreement 1996	Percentage to be paid by the MIB	Time of payment	If decision appealed
Judgment obtained against an identified person, not satisfied in full within 3 months	Apportionment of amount equal to that proportion of a full award attributable to the untraced person	After 3 months	Date of disposal of the appeal
Judgment obtained against the identified person and satisfied in part	(1) If the unsatisfied part of the judgment is less than the proportion of an award payable by the untraced person, the MIB will pay the unsatisfied part (2) If the unsatisfied part of the judgment is equal to or greater than the amount attributable to the untraced person, the MIB will pay the untraced person's proportion	After 3 months	Date of disposal of the appeal
Applicant not required by the MIB to obtain judgment and has not received any compensation from an identified person	An amount equal to the proportion of a full award payable by the untraced person	As soon as the application is quantified by the MIB	

24   Clause 5 of the 1996 Agreement.

Note

If after appeal, the amount ordered to be paid by the identified person is reduced, the above apportionments will be recalculated by the MIB accordingly.

13.5.2 Transcript of proceedings (Clause 6(2))

If the applicant is requested to take proceedings against an identified person, the applicant should provide, if requested, at the MIB's expense, a transcript of any official shorthand note taken in the proceedings of evidence given or judgment delivered.[25]

13.5.3 Assignment of judgment (Clause 6(1)(c))

The applicant must assign any judgment to the MIB where requested to do so in respect of death or injury. The MIB must then account to the applicant if they recover compensation from the identified person.

13.5.4 MIB refusing to indemnify the applicant for proceedings against an identified person

If the MIB refuses to indemnify the applicant for the costs of proceedings against an identified person, it must provide its reasons along with a copy of any transcript, evidence or judgment relevant to its decision.

If the applicant does not accept the MIB's decision, an appeal should be made to an arbitrator[26] (see the appeals section in Chapter 15). The appeal must be made within six weeks of the decision to refuse to indemnify the applicant for the costs of the proceedings against the identified person.

13.6 ASSISTANCE BY THE APPLICANT (CLAUSE 6)

Under the terms of the 1996 Agreement, the applicant must assist the MIB in its enquiries, including providing witness statements, information in writing or orally at interview with the MIB or anyone acting on its behalf. The applicant can be accompanied at interview by a solicitor, although only fixed costs are payable[27] for the handling of the claim. The applicant's solicitor should obtain

---

25 Clause 6(2).
26 See Clause 6(3).
27 See 13.9.

a full and detailed witness statement to support the claim and send this to the MIB with the application form, which may obviate the need for an interview.

13.6.1 Statutory declaration (Clause 8)

If the MIB requests one, the applicant must provide a statutory declaration of the facts and circumstances upon which his application is based, or specific facts and circumstances requested by the MIB. Again, this is subject to the requirement of reasonableness.[28]

13.7 REASONABLENESS OF REQUIREMENTS BY THE MIB (CLAUSE 6(3))

> Letters L25 and L26

Unless the requirement by the MIB relates to the bringing of proceedings against an identified person (in which case, an arbitrator will deal with the matter), the requirement by the MIB is subject to the test of reasonableness, and any issue is determined by the Secretary of State for Transport. There are no published results of referrals to the Secretary of State or the decisions reached by him, although the authors are starting to record decisions made by him through their website,[29] set up to assist those making claims against uninsured and untraced drivers.

If the MIB makes a request for information and/or documentation which those acting on behalf of the applicant consider is not reasonable, notice in writing must be given to the Secretary of State and should be copied to the MIB.[30]

13.8 AWARDS

Awards made will be communicated to the applicant with the following details:

(1) The circumstances in which the death or injury occurred and the relevant evidence.

---

28 See 13.7; Clause 6(3) of the 1996 Agreement.

29 www.mib-help.co.uk.

30 See 7.3, letters L25 and L26.

(2) The circumstances relevant to the assessment of the amount to be awarded and the evidence.

13.8.1 Awards to children/persons not of full capacity (Clause 23)

Where the MIB considers it in the best interests of the applicant to do so, it can arrange for all or part of the award to be paid into a trust and administered by the Family Welfare Association, some other body or person, or by the Court of Protection.

For full protection for the solicitor and the applicant's representative, any award made to a child or person not of full capacity should be approved by the arbitrator. Proceedings normally would be issued under Part 8 of the Civil Procedure Rules, but this cannot be done where no defendant exists.

13.9   COSTS

The 1996 Agreement makes no provision for the payment of any legal costs or disbursements. The payment of £150 for legal costs for the first applicant, and £75 for each one thereafter involved in the same accident represented by the same firm, is provided by an agreement between the Law Society and the MIB. The new Untraced Drivers Agreement, which was initially due to be published early in 2002, but at the time of publication is still awaited, is expected to provide for an increased payment of legal costs. It is understood that this sum will still be well below the amount which would be awarded in the courts for a case of a similar value. This severe limitation on costs is one of the issues currently awaiting consideration by the European Court.[31]

13.9.1   Disbursements

There is no provision for the payment of disbursements. Reasonable disbursements are paid by the MIB, but it will not pay for police accident reports or counsel's fees, although these may be reasonable in approving a settlement for a child/person not of full capacity. There is no right of appeal against an offer for costs or disbursements as there is no provision in the Agreement.

---

31 *Evans v SSETR and MIB* [2001] PIQR 33.

13.10 THE 'ACCELERATED PROCEDURE' (CLAUSES 24–26)

The MIB can (instead of making full investigations and providing a written report on its findings) make an offer to settle the claim under what is known as the 'accelerated procedure'.

When making such an offer, the MIB will provide the applicant with particulars of the circumstances and evidence relating to the injury or death, and the circumstances and evidence used to determine the amount of the award.

If such an offer is not accepted, either negotiations can take place, or a request can be made for a full investigation by the MIB.[32]

---

32 Clause 11(2)(a) of the 1996 Agreement.

CHAPTER 14

PRACTICAL STEPS IN MAKING A CLAIM UNDER THE UNTRACED DRIVERS AGREEMENT

The 1996 Agreement imposes only a few strict time limits, but there is serious potential that the client will already be dangerously close to breaching the Agreement at the time of the first contact with the solicitor. A detailed first interview with all road traffic accident clients is therefore necessary and the following actions must be considered in all cases immediately upon receipt of instructions.[1]

CHAPTER SUMMARY

14.1	**Actions to be taken on receipt of instructions**	☐
14.1.1	Report to the police within 14 days	☐
14.1.2	Application form	☐
14.2	**Issues to consider**	☐
14.2.1	Practical considerations	☐
14.2.2	Children/persons not of full capacity	☐
14.2.3	The passenger applicant	☐
14.2.4	Exceptions	☐
14.3	**Standard letters**	☐
L34	Letter to the client following receipt of instructions	☐
L35	Letter to the police reporting the incident	☐
L36	Letter to the MIB lodging the Untraced Drivers Agreement application form	☐
14.4	**Diary entries**	☐

14.1   ACTIONS TO BE TAKEN ON RECEIPT OF INSTRUCTIONS

Unless you are certain that, at the time the applicant instructs you, the driver is untraced, in addition to the further action detailed below, all actions and

---

1   See also Chapter 4 where the driver may be uninsured or untraced.

procedures set out in Chapter 4 must be considered and applied. In addition, the following specific action must be taken under the 1996 Agreement.

14.1.1 Report to the police within 14 days

Letters L34 and L35

The 1996 Agreement provides that the accident must be reported to the police within 14 days or as soon as the applicant reasonably could and the applicant co-operated with the police in the course of their enquiries. As soon as you are consulted regarding any accident claim, send letter L34 to your client.

14.1.2 Application form

Letter L36

As proceedings cannot be issued, the application form to proceed under the Untraced Drivers Agreement must be lodged within three years of the date of the accident.[2] Lodge the application form with the MIB and request confirmation that the claim is proceeding under the Untraced Drivers Agreement. This action should be taken even if the claim is likely to proceed against a possibly identified party and the untraced driver (that is, where more than one party is at fault).[3]

The MIB has taken to attaching a form of authority to the application form for the release of all medical records, employment records, DSS and insurance records. See 7.2 for action to be considered if you do not think it is reasonable for the MIB to receive such information.

14.2   ISSUES TO CONSIDER

14.2.1   Practical considerations

The MIB will carry out all of the investigations, interview your client, obtain its own medical evidence and make an offer. The applicant's solicitor has to be able to advise on the appropriateness of the offer within the six weeks available

---

2   See 14.4, diary entries.
3   See 13.5.

to appeal a decision. Therefore, an applicant's solicitor should ensure that any evidence needed to assess an offer is available prior to an application being finally considered by the MIB.

14.2.2 Children/persons not of full capacity

See 13.4.1.

14.2.3 The passenger applicant

```
Questionnaire Q1
```

If the client was a passenger in a vehicle which was being driven by the untraced driver, various exceptions need to be carefully considered, as he may not be entitled to any damages. See 13.4.2. The questionnaire at 4.4 (Q1) should be completed to enable a full statement to be drafted dealing with the relevant points at a very early stage: this is likely to be one of the first issues that the MIB will wish to deal with and therefore will potentially hold up the making of an award at all, or the time when the award is finally made. See 4.2.2.1 to 4.2.2.3 for further consideration of passenger exclusions.

14.2.4 Exceptions

See 13.4.3 and 4.2.3.

14.3   STANDARD LETTERS

L34   Letter to the client following receipt of instructions

Client address

Dear

Accident date:

I confirm that I have asked you to attend the local police station and report to them immediately the accident in which you were injured. This action is essential. If the identity of the other driver is subsequently discovered to be false, the claim would be dealt with by the Motor Insurers' Bureau (the MIB), which compensates victims of untraced and uninsured drivers.

The MIB can refuse to compensate you if you fail to notify the police within 14 days of the date of the incident and if you fail to co-operate fully with the police in the course of their enquiries. Therefore, you must notify the police immediately if you have not already done so. Please ensure that you obtain an accident reference number, or at the very least the name of the officer you report the incident to, and forward these details to me.

Yours

L35   Letter to the police reporting the incident

BY FAX/RECORDED DELIVERY ONLY FOR PROOF OF RECEIPT:

Dear

Our client:
Accident date:
Other driver's name:

Our client was involved in an accident with the above-named third party on the above date.

Our client sustained injury and losses, and we are instructed to pursue a claim for damages on behalf of our client.

The details of the accident are as follows:

(Insert location, date, time, full circumstances)

We would ask you to fully investigate the incident and attempt to locate the driver of the other vehicle. Details we hold in relation to that other driver are as follows:

(Insert any known name, address, vehicle registration number and circumstances for failing to obtain full details)

We confirm our client will co-operate fully with all enquiries and our client's details are as follows:

(Name, address, telephone)

We look forward to hearing from you.

Yours

L36   Letter to the MIB lodging the Untraced Drivers Agreement application form

BY FAX/RECORDED DELIVERY:

Dear

Client name:
Accident date:
Untraced driver:

We are proceeding with a claim under the 1996 Untraced Drivers Agreement. Please find enclosed the Untraced Drivers Agreement application form and confirm that you accept that the claim is proceeding under the terms of the 1996 Untraced Drivers Agreement.

Yours

14.4 DIARY ENTRIES

Document reference	Description	Number of days
L34	Short letter to the client setting out requirement to notify the police and co-operate with enquiries	As soon as instructions are received
L35	Letter to the police notifying them of the incident	As soon as instructions are received
L36	Lodge Untraced Drivers Agreement application form	28 days and strictly no later than 3 years from the accident date[4]
	Written confirmation from the MIB that it has accepted the claim under the Untraced Drivers Agreement and is investigating	Every 28 days from the date of the lodging of the application

4   See 13.4.1.

CHAPTER 15

APPEALS UNDER THE UNTRACED DRIVERS AGREEMENT

CHAPTER SUMMARY

15.1	**Time for appeals**	☐
15.2	**Practical considerations before appeal**	☐
15.2.1	Negotiation	☐
15.2.2	Cost	☐
15.2.3	Further evidence	☐
15.3	**Appeals against insufficient awards**	☐
15.4	**Submission of appeals to the arbitrator**	☐
15.5	**Requests by the arbitrator for further investigation**	☐
15.6	**Possible outcomes of appeals**	☐
15.7	**Costs of appeals**	☐
15.8	**Standard letters**	☐
L37	Letter to the MIB appealing the decision	☐
L38	Undertaking to be sent with the letter enclosing the appeal	☐
15.9	**Diary entries**	☐

15.1   TIME FOR APPEALS

Letters L37 and L38

Upon receipt of the award, the applicant has only six weeks to appeal against the decision. It is therefore important that any evidence collected by the applicant is prepared into an appropriate appeal bundle and a full appeal is lodged with the MIB within the six week period.[1]

---

1   See letters L37 and L38.

15.2 PRACTICAL CONSIDERATIONS BEFORE APPEAL

15.2.1 Negotiation

It may not be necessary to formally appeal against the decision of the MIB as the matter may be capable of resolution by negotiation.

15.2.2 Cost

The cost of the arbitrator is normally in the region of £450 and can be ordered to be paid by the applicant. Questions of proportionality will have to be considered. If the difference in the amount offered and the amount sought by the applicant is minimal, telephone negotiations often lead to the successful conclusion of the application without the need and expense of the appeal.

15.2.3 Further evidence

Any further evidence obtained since the application was lodged, relating either to the decision not to make an award or the amount awarded (that is, further medical evidence), should be forwarded to the MIB as soon as possible in an attempt to reach a satisfactory conclusion before appealing.

Even after an appeal has been lodged by the applicant, the MIB can decide to make further investigations and report the results of those investigations to the applicant.[2]

Once again, any further offer put forward by the MIB after the receipt of documents for an appeal, but before it is forwarded to an arbitrator, must be accepted or appealed within six weeks.[3]

15.3 APPEALS AGAINST INSUFFICIENT AWARDS

Once an appeal has been lodged against an insufficient award, the MIB can give notice to the applicant that it will ask the arbitrator to decide whether an award should be made at all under the terms of the 1996 Agreement and will supply the applicant with a statement of issues relating to that request to the arbitrator.[4] In practice, if the MIB has already decided to make an award under the terms of the 1996 Agreement, it is unlikely that an arbitrator will change that decision.

---

2   Clause 13(2) of the 1996 Agreement.
3   Clause 13(3) of the 1996 Agreement.
4   Clause 14(1) of the 1996 Agreement.

The applicant is once again given six weeks to provide a statement of further issues in response to the one from the MIB, which the arbitrator will consider with the appeal.

Once the applicant has provided a statement of issues, the MIB can decide again to change its initial award before lodging the papers with the arbitrator.[5] The applicant will again have six weeks to accept or reject the offer made.

15.4   SUBMISSION OF APPEALS TO THE ARBITRATOR

If the MIB decides to submit the papers to an arbitrator, it will send:

(a) the application;

(b) a copy of the MIB's decision;

(c) copies of all statements, declarations, notices, undertakings, comments, transcripts and particulars of reports provided by the applicant or the MIB.

15.5   REQUESTS BY THE ARBITRATOR FOR FURTHER INVESTIGATION

Before making a decision, the MIB can be requested by the arbitrator to make further enquiries and provide a written report to him. Before submitting the written report to the arbitrator, a copy of it must be sent to the applicant, who then has four weeks from the date the MIB sent[6] the written report to him to send any written comments to the MIB that he wants the arbitrator to consider.

---

5   Clause 14(2) of the 1996 Agreement.

6   Note that Clause 17(2) of the 1996 Agreement states that the written comments must be sent to the MIB within four weeks of the date that the MIB sent its report to the applicant, *not* within four weeks of *receipt* of that report by the applicant.

15.6   POSSIBLE OUTCOMES OF APPEALS

Decision appealed	Outcome 1	Outcome 2
Rejection of an application under the 1996 Agreement	The arbitrator agrees with the MIB's decision to reject the application	The arbitrator decides an award should be made and returns the papers to the MIB to fully investigate and make an award (all terms of the 1996 Agreement apply)[7]
Insufficient award	The arbitrator agrees with the MIB's decision of the amount offered	The arbitrator disagrees with the MIB and orders more or less to be paid to the applicant
Refusal to indemnify the applicant for the costs of proceedings against an identified person	The arbitrator agrees with the MIB's decision not to indemnify	The arbitrator disagrees with the MIB's decision and the MIB indemnifies the applicant

The decision is sent to the MIB, and then the MIB sends it on to the applicant, along with any payment ordered to be made to the applicant.

15.7   COSTS OF APPEALS

No costs of either the MIB or the applicant are payable, but the arbitrator's fees can be ordered to be paid by the applicant if the arbitrator believes there were no reasonable grounds for the appeal. As stated earlier, these costs are normally in the region of £450 and can be deducted from any award to be paid by the MIB to the applicant.

---

7   Clause 16 of the 1996 Agreement. If an application is first rejected, but on appeal the MIB is ordered to investigate and make an award, the application is in effect treated as a new application and all terms of the 1996 Agreement will apply.

15.8   STANDARD LETTERS

L37   Letter to the MIB appealing the decision

Motor Insurers' Bureau
[Registered Office]

BY RECORDED DELIVERY:

Dear

Applicant:
Accident date:

We refer to your letter of *(insert date)* notifying us of your decision to *(insert decision)*.

This letter constitutes the applicant's notice of appeal against that decision.

EITHER:

The grounds for the appeal are:

> *(Insert grounds of appeal)*

The following documents are provided in support of the appeal:

> *(Insert list of documents)*

OR:

We enclose the duly completed MIB appeal form.

Please acknowledge receipt.

Yours

L38   Undertaking to be sent with the letter enclosing the appeal

Solicitor's reference:

MIB reference:

UNDERTAKING

In accordance with Clause 12 of the Motor Insurers' Bureau (Compensation of Victims of Untraced Drivers) Agreement 1996, I *(name of client)* of *(address)* undertake that I will accept as final the decision of the Arbitrator regarding my appeal.

Signed: ....

Print name: ....

15.9   DIARY ENTRIES

Document reference	Description	Number of days
L37 and L38	Appeal against an insufficient award	Lodge within 6 weeks of the date that the MIB *sent*[8] the notice to the applicant
L37 and L38	Appeal against rejection of application	Lodge within 6 weeks of the date that the MIB *sent* the notice to the applicant
L37 and L38	Appeal against an increased offer made after lodging the initial appeal	Lodge within 6 weeks of the date that the MIB *sent* the notice to the applicant
	The arbitrator asks the MIB to make further investigations before determining an appeal, and copies of the subsequent report are sent to the applicant	Serve written comments on the MIB within four weeks of the date the MIB *sent*[9] the notice to the applicant

---

8   Note that Clause 15(2) of the 1996 Agreement states that the appeal is to be lodged within six weeks of the date the MIB sent the notice of award/rejection/increased offer, *not* within six weeks of *receipt* of that notice by the applicant.

9   Note that Clause 17(2) of the 1996 Agreement states that the written comments must be sent to the MIB within four weeks of the date the MIB sent its report to the applicant, *not* within four weeks of *receipt* of that report by the applicant.

THE UNINSURED DRIVERS AGREEMENT 1999 AND THE ORIGINAL NOTES FOR GUIDANCE

13th August 1999

MOTOR INSURERS' BUREAU (COMPENSATION OF VICTIMS OF UNINSURED DRIVERS)

Text of an Agreement dated the 13th August 1999 between the Secretary of State for the Environment, Transport and the Regions and Motor Insurers' Bureau together with some notes on its scope and purpose

THIS AGREEMENT is made the thirteenth day of August 1999 between the SECRETARY OF STATE FOR THE ENVIRONMENT, TRANSPORT AND THE REGIONS (hereinafter referred to as 'the Secretary of State') and the MOTOR INSURERS' BUREAU, whose registered office is at 152 Silbury Boulevard, Milton Keynes MK9 1NB (hereinafter referred to as 'MIB') and is SUPPLEMENTAL to an Agreement (hereinafter called 'the Principal Agreement') made the 31st day of December 1945 between the Minister of War Transport and the insurers transacting compulsory motor insurance business in Great Britain by or on behalf of whom the said Agreement was signed and in pursuance of paragraph 1 of which MIB was incorporated.

IT IS HEREBY AGREED AS FOLLOWS:

INTERPRETATION

General definitions

1   In this Agreement, unless the context otherwise requires, the following expressions have the following meanings –

'1988 Act' means the Road Traffic Act 1988;

'1988 Agreement' means the Agreement made on 21 December 1988 between the Secretary of State for Transport and MIB;

'bank holiday' means a day which is, or is to be observed as, a bank holiday under the Banking and Financial Dealings Act 1971;

'claimant' means a person who has commenced or who proposes to commence relevant proceedings and has made an application under this Agreement in respect thereof;

'contract of insurance' means a policy of insurance or a security covering a relevant liability;

'insurer' includes the giver of a security;

'MIB's obligation' means the obligation contained in Clause 5;

'property' means any property whether real, heritable or personal;

'relevant liability' means a liability in respect of which a contract of insurance must be in force to comply with Part VI of the 1988 Act;

'relevant proceedings' means proceedings in respect of a relevant liability (and 'commencement', in relation to such proceedings means, in England and Wales, the date on which a Claim Form or other originating process is issued by a Court or, in Scotland, the date on which the originating process is served on the Defender);

'relevant sum' means a sum payable or remaining payable under an unsatisfied judgment, including –

(a) an amount payable or remaining payable in respect of interest on that sum; and

(b) either the whole of the costs (whether taxed or not) awarded by the Court as part of that judgment or, where the judgment includes an award in respect of a liability which is not a relevant liability, such proportion of those costs as the relevant liability bears to the total sum awarded under the judgment;

'specified excess' means £300 or such other sum as may from time to time be agreed in writing between the Secretary of State and MIB;

'unsatisfied judgment' means a judgment or order (by whatever name called) in respect of a relevant liability which has not been satisfied in full within seven days from the date upon which the claimant became entitled to enforce it.

Meaning of references

2.1 Save as otherwise herein provided, the Interpretation Act 1978 shall apply for the interpretation of this Agreement as it applies for the interpretation of an Act of Parliament.

2.2 Where, under this Agreement, something is required to be done –

(a) within a specified period after or from the happening of a particular event, the period begins on the day after the happening of that event;

(b) within or not less than a specified period before a particular event, the period ends on the day immediately before the happening of that event.

2.3 Where, apart from this paragraph, the period in question, being a period of seven days or less, would include a Saturday, Sunday or bank holiday or Christmas Day or Good Friday, that day shall be excluded.

2.4 Save where expressly otherwise provided, a reference in this Agreement to a numbered Clause is a reference to the Clause bearing that number in this Agreement and a reference to a numbered paragraph is a reference to a paragraph bearing that number in the Clause in which the reference occurs.

2.5 In this Agreement –

(a) a reference (however framed) to the doing of any act or thing by or the happening of any event in relation to the claimant includes a reference to the doing of that act or thing by or the happening of that event in relation to a Solicitor or other person acting on his behalf, and

(b) a requirement to give notice to, or to serve documents upon, MIB or an insurer mentioned in Clause 9(1)(a) shall be satisfied by the giving of the notice to, or the service of the documents upon, a Solicitor acting on its behalf in the manner provided for.

Claimants not of full age or capacity

3.1 Where, under and in accordance with this Agreement –

(a) any act or thing is done to or by a Solicitor or other person acting on behalf of a claimant;

(b) any decision is made by or in respect of a Solicitor or other person acting on behalf of a claimant; or

(c) any sum is paid to a Solicitor or other person acting on behalf of a claimant, then, whatever may be the age or other circumstances affecting the capacity of the claimant, that act, thing, decision or sum shall be treated as if it had been done to or by, or made in respect of or paid to a claimant of full age and capacity.

PRINCIPAL TERMS

Duration of Agreement

4.1 This Agreement shall come into force on 1st October 1999 in relation to accidents occurring on or after that date and, save as provided by Clause 23, the 1988 Agreement shall cease and determine immediately before that date.

4.2 This Agreement may be determined by the Secretary of State or by MIB giving to the other not less than twelve months' notice in writing but without prejudice to its continued operation in respect of accidents occurring before the date of termination.

MIB's obligation to satisfy compensation claims

5.1   Subject to Clauses 6 to 17, if a claimant has obtained against any person in a Court in Great Britain a judgment which is an unsatisfied judgment then MIB will pay the relevant sum to, or to the satisfaction of, the claimant or will cause the same to be so paid.

5.2   Paragraph (1) applies whether or not the person liable to satisfy the judgment is in fact covered by a contract of insurance and whatever may be the cause of his failure to satisfy the judgment.

EXCEPTIONS TO AGREEMENT

6.1   Clause 5 does not apply in the case of an application made in respect of a claim of any of the following descriptions (and, where part only of a claim satisfies such a description, Clause 5 does not apply to that part) –

(a)   a claim arising out of a relevant liability incurred by the user of a vehicle owned by or in the possession of the Crown, unless –
  (i)   responsibility for the existence of a contract of insurance under Part VI of the 1988 Act in relation to that vehicle had been undertaken by some other person (whether or not the person liable was in fact covered by a contract of insurance), or
  (ii)   the relevant liability was in fact covered by a contract of insurance;
(b)   a claim arising out of the use of a vehicle which is not required to be covered by a contract of insurance by virtue of section 144 of the 1988 Act, unless the use is in fact covered by such a contract;
(c)   a claim by, or for the benefit of, a person ('the beneficiary') other than the person suffering death, injury or other damage which is made either –
  (i)   in respect of a cause of action or a judgment which has been assigned to the beneficiary, or
  (ii)   pursuant to a right of subrogation or contractual or other right belonging to the beneficiary;
(d)   a claim in respect of damage to a motor vehicle or losses arising therefrom where, at the time when the damage to it was sustained –
  (i)   there was not in force in relation to the use of that vehicle such a contract of insurance as is required by Part VI of the 1988 Act, and
  (ii)   the claimant either knew or ought to have known that that was the case;
(e)   a claim which is made in respect of a relevant liability described in paragraph (2) by a claimant who, at the time of the use giving rise to the relevant liability was voluntarily allowing himself to be carried in the vehicle and, either before the commencement of his journey in the vehicle or after such commencement if he could reasonably be expected to have alighted from it, knew or ought to have known that –

(i)   the vehicle had been stolen or unlawfully taken,

(ii)   the vehicle was being used without there being in force in relation to its use such a contract of insurance as would comply with Part VI of the 1988 Act,

(iii) the vehicle was being used in the course or furtherance of a crime, or

(iv)   the vehicle was being used as a means of escape from, or avoidance of, lawful apprehension.

6.2   The relevant liability referred to in paragraph (1)(e) is a liability incurred by the owner or registered keeper or a person using the vehicle in which the claimant was being carried.

6.3   The burden of proving that the claimant knew or ought to have known of any matter set out in paragraph (1)(e) shall be on MIB but, in the absence of evidence to the contrary, proof by MIB of any of the following matters shall be taken as proof of the claimant's knowledge of the matter set out in paragraph (1)(e)(ii) –

(a)   that the claimant was the owner or registered keeper of the vehicle or had caused or permitted its use;

(b)   that the claimant knew the vehicle was being used by a person who was below the minimum age at which he could be granted a licence authorising the driving of a vehicle of that class;

(c)   that the claimant knew that the person driving the vehicle was disqualified for holding or obtaining a driving licence;

(d)   that the claimant knew that the user of the vehicle was neither its owner nor registered keeper nor an employee of the owner or registered keeper nor the owner or registered keeper of any other vehicle.

6.4   Knowledge which the claimant has or ought to have for the purposes of paragraph (1)(e) includes knowledge of matters which he could reasonably be expected to have been aware of had he not been under the self-induced influence of drink or drugs.

6.5   For the purposes of this Clause –

(a)   a vehicle which has been unlawfully removed from the possession of the Crown shall be taken to continue in that possession whilst it is kept so removed;

(b)   references to a person being carried in a vehicle include references to his being carried upon, entering, getting on to and alighting from the vehicle; and

(c)   'owner', in relation to a vehicle which is the subject of a hiring agreement or a hire-purchase agreement, means the person in possession of the vehicle under that agreement.

CONDITIONS PRECEDENT TO MIB'S OBLIGATION

Form of application

7.1 MIB shall incur no liability under MIB's obligation unless an application is made to the person specified in Clause 9(1) –

(a)   in such form;
(b)   giving such information about the relevant proceedings and other matters relevant to this Agreement; and
(c)   accompanied by such documents as MIB may reasonably require.

7.2 Where an application is signed by a person who is neither the claimant nor a Solicitor acting on his behalf MIB may refuse to accept the application (and shall incur no liability under MIB's obligation) until it is reasonably satisfied that, having regard to the status of the signatory and his relationship to the claimant, the claimant is fully aware of the contents and effect of the application but subject thereto MIB shall not refuse to accept such an application by reason only that it is signed by a person other than the claimant or his Solicitor.

Service of notices, etc

8.1 Any notice required to be given or documents to be supplied to MIB pursuant to Clauses 9 to 12 of this Agreement shall be sufficiently given or supplied only if sent by facsimile transmission or by Registered or Recorded Delivery post to MIB's registered office for the time being and delivery shall be proved by the production of a facsimile transmission report produced by the sender's facsimile machine or an appropriate postal receipt.

Notice of relevant proceedings

9.1 MIB shall incur no liability under MIB's obligation unless proper notice of the bringing of the relevant proceedings has been given by the claimant not later than 14 days after the commencement of those proceedings –

(a)   in the case of proceedings in respect of a relevant liability which is covered by a contract of insurance with an insurer whose identity can be ascertained, to that insurer;
(b)   in any other case, to MIB.

9.2 In this Clause 'proper notice' means, except insofar as any part of such information or any copy document or other thing has already been supplied under Clause 7 –

(a)   notice in writing that proceedings have been commenced by Claim Form, Writ, or other means;

(b)   a copy of the sealed Claim Form, Writ or other official document providing evidence of the commencement of the proceedings and, in Scotland, a statement of the means of service;

(c)   a copy or details of any insurance policy providing benefits in the case of the death, bodily injury or damage to property to which the proceedings relate where the claimant is the insured party and the benefits are available to him;

(d)   copies of all correspondence in the possession of the claimant or (as the case may be) his Solicitor or agent to or from the Defendant or the Defender or (as the case may be) his Solicitor, insurers or agent which is relevant to –

    (i)   the death, bodily in jury or damage for which the Defendant or Defender is alleged to be responsible, or

    (ii)   any contract of insurance which covers, or which may or has been alleged to cover, liability for such death, injury or damage the benefit of which is, or is claimed to be, available to the Defendant or Defender;

(e)   subject to paragraph (3), a copy of the Particulars of Claim whether or not indorsed on the Claim Form, Writ or other originating process, and whether or not served (in England and Wales) on any Defendant or (in Scotland) on any Defender; and

(f)   a copy of all other documents which are required under the appropriate rules of procedure to be served on a Defendant or Defender with the Claim Form, Writ or other originating process or with the Particulars of Claim;

(g)   such other information about the relevant proceedings as MIB may reasonably specify.

9.3 If, in the case of proceedings commenced in England or Wales, the Particulars of Claim (including any document required to be served therewith) has not yet been served with the Claim Form or other originating process paragraph (2)(e) shall be sufficiently complied with if a copy thereof is served on MIB not later than seven days after it is served on the Defendant.

Notice of service of proceedings

10.1 This Clause applies where the relevant proceedings are commenced in England or Wales.

10.2 MIB shall incur no liability under MIB's obligation unless the claimant has, not later than the appropriate date, given notice in writing to the person specified in Clause 9(1) of the date of service of the Claim Form or other originating process in the relevant proceedings.

10.3 In this Clause, 'the appropriate date' means the day falling –

(a)   seven days after –

    (i)   the date when the claimant receives notification from the Court that service of the Claim Form or other originating process has occurred,

(ii) the date when the claimant receives notification from the Defendant that service of the Claim Form or other originating process has occurred, or

(iii) the date of personal service, or

(b) 14 days after the date when service is deemed to have occurred in accordance with the Civil Procedure Rules, whichever of those days occurs first.

Further information

11.1 MIB shall incur no liability under MIB's obligation unless the claimant has, not later than seven days after the occurrence of any of the following events, namely –

(a) the filing of a defence in the relevant proceedings,

(b) any amendment to the Particulars of Claim or any amendment of or addition to any schedule or other document required to be served therewith; and

(c) either –

(i) the setting down of the case for trial, or

(ii) where the court gives notice to the claimant of the trial date, the date when that notice is received, given notice in writing of the date of that event to the person specified in Clause 9(1) and has, in the case of the filing of a defence or an amendment of the Particulars of Claim or any amendment of or addition to any schedule or other document required to be served therewith, supplied a copy thereof to that person.

11.2 MIB shall incur no liability under MIB's obligation unless the claimant furnishes to the person specified in Clause 9(1) within a reasonable time after being required to do so such further information and documents in support of his claim as MIB may reasonably require notwithstanding that the claimant may have complied with Clause 7(1).

Notice of intention to apply for judgment

12.1 MIB shall incur no liability under MIB's obligation unless the claimant has, after commencement of the relevant proceedings and not less than 35 days before the appropriate date, given notice in writing to the person specified in Clause 9(1) of his intention to apply for or to sign judgment in the relevant proceedings.

12.2 In this Clause, 'the appropriate date' means the date when the application for judgment is made or, as the case may be, the signing of judgment occurs.

Section 154 of the 1988 Act

13.1 MIB shall incur no liability under MIB's obligation unless the claimant has as soon as reasonably practicable –

(a) demanded the information and, where appropriate, the particulars specified in section 154(1) of the 1988 Act; and
(b) if the person of whom the demand is made fails to comply with the provisions of that subsection –
  (i) made a formal complaint to a police officer in respect of such failure, and
  (ii) used all reasonable endeavours to obtain the name and address of the registered keeper of the vehicle or, if so required by MIB, has authorised MIB to take such steps on his behalf.

Prosecution of proceedings

14.1 MIB shall incur no liability under MIB's obligation –

(a) unless the claimant has, if so required by MIB and having been granted a full indemnity by MIB as to costs, taken all reasonable steps to obtain judgment against every person who may be liable (including any person who may be vicariously liable) in respect of the injury or death or damage to property; or
(b) if the claimant, upon being requested to do so by MIB, refuses to consent to MIB being joined as a party to the relevant proceedings.

Assignment of judgment and undertakings

15.1 MIB shall incur no liability under MIB's obligation unless the claimant has –

(a) assigned to MIB or its nominee the unsatisfied judgment, whether or not that judgment includes an amount in respect of a liability other than a relevant liability, and any order for costs made in the relevant proceedings; and
(b) undertaken to repay to MIB any sum paid to him –
  (i) by MIB in discharge of MIB's obligation if the judgment is subsequently set aside either as a whole or in respect of the part of the relevant liability to which that sum relates,
  (ii) by any other person by way of compensation or benefit for the death, bodily injury or other damage to which the relevant proceedings relate, including a sum which would have been deductible under the provisions of Clause 17 if it had been received before MIB was obliged to satisfy MIB's obligation.

LIMITATIONS ON MIB'S LIABILITY

Compensation for damage to property

16.1 Where a claim under this Agreement includes a claim in respect of damage to property, MIB's obligation in respect of that part of the relevant sum which is awarded for such damage and any losses arising therefrom (referred to in this Clause as 'the property damage compensation') is limited in accordance with the following paragraphs.

16.2 Where the property damage compensation does not exceed the specified excess, MIB shall incur no liability.

16.3 Where the property damage compensation in respect of any one accident exceeds the specified excess but does not exceed £250,000, MIB shall incur liability less the specified excess.

16.4 Where the property damage compensation in respect of any one accident exceeds £250,000, MIB shall incur liability only in respect of the sum of £250,000 less the specified excess.

Compensation received from other sources

17.1 Where a claimant has received compensation from –

(a) the Policyholders Protection Board under the Policyholders Protection Act 1975; or
(b) an insurer under an insurance agreement or arrangement; or
(c) any other source, in respect of the death, bodily injury or other damage to which the relevant proceedings relate and such compensation has not been taken into account in the calculation of the relevant sum MIB may deduct from the relevant sum, in addition to any sum deductible under Clause 16, an amount equal to that compensation.

MISCELLANEOUS

Notifications of decisions by MIB

18.1 Where a claimant –

(a) has made an application in accordance with Clause 7, and
(b) has given to the person specified in Clause 9(1) proper notice of the relevant proceedings in accordance with Clause 9(2), MIB shall –
   (i)   give a reasoned reply to any request made by the claimant relating to the payment of compensation in pursuance of MIB's obligation, and

(ii) as soon as reasonably practicable notify the claimant in writing of its decision regarding the payment of the relevant sum, together with the reasons for that decision.

Reference of disputes to the Secretary of State

19.1 In the event of any dispute as to the reasonableness of a requirement made by MIB for the supply of information or documentation or for the taking of any step by the claimant, it may be referred by the claimant or MIB to the Secretary of State whose decision shall be final.

19.2 Where a dispute is referred to the Secretary of State –

(a) MIB shall supply the Secretary of State and, if it has not already done so, the claimant with notice in writing of the requirement from which the dispute arises, together with the reasons for that requirement and such further information as MIB considers relevant; and

(b) where the dispute is referred by the claimant, the claimant shall supply the Secretary of State and, if he has not already done so, MIB with notice in writing of the grounds on which he disputes the reasonableness of the requirement.

Recoveries

20.1 Nothing in this Agreement shall prevent an insurer from providing by conditions in a contract of insurance that all sums paid by the insurer or by MIB by virtue of the Principal Agreement or this Agreement in or towards the discharge of the liability of the insured shall be recoverable by them or by MIB from the insured or from any other person.

Apportionment of damages, etc

21.1 Where an unsatisfied judgment which includes an amount in respect of a liability other than a relevant liability has been assigned to MIB or its nominee in pursuance of Clause 15 MIB shall –

(a) apportion any sum it receives in satisfaction or partial satisfaction of the judgment according to the proportion which the damages awarded in respect of the relevant liability bear to the damages awarded in respect of the other liability; and

(b) account to the claimant in respect of the moneys received properly apportionable to the other liability.

21.2 Where the sum received includes an amount in respect of interest or an amount awarded under an order for costs, the interest or the amount received in pursuance of the order shall be dealt with in the manner provided in paragraph (1).

Agents

22.1 MIB may perform any of its obligations under this agreement by agents.

Transitional provisions

23.1 The 1988 Agreement shall continue in force in relation to claims arising out of accidents occurring before 1st October 1999 with the modifications contained in paragraph (2).

23.2 In relation to any claim made under the 1988 Agreement after this Agreement has come into force, the 1988 Agreement shall apply as if there were inserted after Clause 6 thereof –

6A Where any person in whose favour a judgment in respect of a relevant liability has been made has –

(a) made a claim under this Agreement, and

(b) satisfied the requirements specified in Clause 5 hereof,

MIB shall, if requested to do so, give him a reasoned reply regarding the satisfaction of that claim.

IN WITNESS whereof the Secretary of State has caused his Corporate Seal to be hereunto affixed and the Motor Insurers' Bureau has caused its Common Seal to be hereunto affixed the day and year first above written.

THE CORPORATE SEAL of the
SECRETARY OF STATE FOR THE
ENVIRONMENT, TRANSPORT AND
THE REGIONS hereunto affixed is
authenticated by:

Authorised by the Secretary of State

THE COMMON SEAL of the MOTOR INSURERS'
BUREAU was hereunto affixed in the presence of:

Directors of the Board of Management
Secretary

ORIGINAL NOTES FOR THE GUIDANCE
OF VICTIMS OF ROAD TRAFFIC ACCIDENTS

The following notes are for the guidance of anyone who may have a claim on the Motor Insurers' Bureau under this Agreement and their legal advisers. They are not part of the Agreement, their purpose being to deal in ordinary language with the situations which most readily occur. They are not in any way a substitute for reading and applying the terms of this or any other relevant Agreement, nor are they intended to control or influence the legal interpretation of the Agreement. These notes vary from the original as they have been updated to reflect recent developments. Any enquiries, requests for application forms and general correspondence in connection with the Agreement should be addressed to:

Motor Insurers' Bureau
152 Silbury Boulevard
Central Milton Keynes
Milton Keynes
MK9 1NB

Tel: 01908 830001
Fax: 01908 671681
DX: 84753 Milton Keynes 3

1 Introduction – MIB's role and application of the Agreement

1.1 The role of MIB under this Agreement is to provide a safety net for innocent victims of drivers who have been identified but are uninsured. MIB's funds for this purpose are obtained from levies charged upon insurers and so come from the premiums which are charged by those insurers to members of the public.

1.2 MIB has entered into a series of Agreements with the Secretary of State and his predecessors in office. Under each Agreement MIB undertakes obligations to pay defined compensation in specific circumstances. There are two sets of Agreements, one relating to victims of uninsured drivers (the 'Uninsured Drivers' Agreements) and the other concerned with victims of hit and run or otherwise untraceable drivers (the 'Untraced Drivers' Agreements). These Notes are addressed specifically to the procedures required to take advantage of the rights granted by the Uninsured Drivers Agreements. However, it is not always certain which of the Agreements applies. For guidance in such cases please see the note on Untraced Drivers at paragraph 11 below.

1.3 In order to determine which of the Uninsured Drivers Agreements is applicable to a particular victim's claim, regard must be had to the date of the relevant accident. This Agreement only applies in respect of claims arising on or after 1st October 1999. Claims arising earlier than that are covered by the following Agreements:

(a) Claims arising in respect of an incident occurring between 1st July 1946 and 28th February 1971 are governed by the Agreement between the Minister of Transport and the Bureau dated 17th June 1946.

(b) Claims arising in respect of an incident occurring between 1st March 1971 and 30th November 1972 are governed by the Agreement between the Secretary of State for the Environment and the Bureau dated 1st February 1971.

(c) Claims arising in respect of an incident occurring between 1st December 1972 and 30th December 1988 are governed by the Agreement between the Secretary of State and the Bureau dated 22nd November 1972.

(d) Claims arising in respect of an incident occurring between 31st December 1988 and 30th September 1999 are governed by the Agreement between the Secretary of State and the Bureau dated 21st December 1988.

2 MIB's obligation

2.1 MIB's basic obligation (see Clause 5) is to satisfy judgments which fall within the terms of this Agreement and which, because the Defendant to the proceedings is not insured, are not satisfied.

2.2 This obligation is, however, not absolute. It is subject to certain exceptions where MIB has no liability (see Clause 6), there are a number of pre-conditions which the claimant must comply with (see Clauses 7 to 15) and there are some limitations on MIB's liability (see Clauses 16 and 17).

2.3 MIB does not have to wait for a judgment to be given; it can become party to the proceedings or negotiate and settle the claim if it wishes to do so.

3 Claims which MIB is not obliged to satisfy

MIB is not liable under the Agreement in the case of the following types of claim.

3.1 A claim made in respect of an unsatisfied judgment which does not concern a liability against which Part VI of the Road Traffic Act 1988 requires a vehicle user to insure (see section 145 of the Act). An example would be a case where the accident did not occur in a place specified in the Act. See the definitions of 'unsatisfied judgment' and 'relevant liability' in Clause 1.

3.2 A claim in respect of loss or damage caused by the use of a vehicle owned by or in the possession of the Crown (that is the Civil Service, the armed forces and so on) to which Part VI does not apply. If the responsibility for motor insurance has been undertaken by someone else or the vehicle is in fact insured, this exception does not apply. See Clause 6(1)(a).

3.3 A claim made against any person who is not required to insure by virtue of section 144 of the Road Traffic Act 1988. See Clause 6(1)(b).

3.4 A claim (commonly called subrogated) made in the name of a person suffering damage or injury but which is in fact wholly or partly for the benefit or another who has indemnified, or is liable to indemnify that person. See Clause 6(1)(c).

3.5 A claim in respect of damage to a motor vehicle or losses arising from such damage where the use of the damaged vehicle was itself not covered by a contract of insurance as required by law. See Clause 6(1)(d).

3.6 A claim made by a passenger in a vehicle where the loss or damage has been caused by the user of that vehicle if:

(a) the use of the vehicle was not covered by a contract of insurance; and

(b) the claimant knew or could be taken to have known that the vehicle was being used without insurance, had been stolen or unlawfully taken or was being used in connection with crime. See Clause 6(1)(e), (2), (3) and (4).

3.7 A claim in respect of property damage amounting to £300 or less, £300 being the 'specified excess'. See Clause 16(2).

3.8 Where the claim is for property damage, the first £300 of the loss and so much of it as exceeds £250,000. See Clause 16(3) and 16(4).

4 Procedure after the accident and before proceedings

4.1 The claimant must take reasonable steps to establish whether there is in fact any insurance covering the use of the vehicle which caused the injury or damage. First, a claimant has statutory rights under section 154 of the Road Traffic Act 1988 to obtain relevant particulars which he must take steps to exercise even if that involves incurring expense and MIB will insist that he does so. See Clause 13(a).

4.2 Other steps will include the following:

(a) The exchange of names, addresses and insurance particulars between those involved either at the scene of the accident or afterwards.

(b) Corresponding with the owner or driver of the vehicle or his representatives. He will be obliged under the terms of his motor policy to inform his insurers and a letter of claim addressed to him will commonly be passed to the insurers who may reply on his behalf. See Clause 9(2)(d).

(c) Where only the vehicle's number is known, enquiry of the Driver and Vehicle Licensing Agency at Swansea SA99 1BP as to the registered keeper of the vehicle is desirable so that through him the identity of the owner or driver can be established or confirmed.

(d) Enquiries of the police (see Clause 13(b)).

4.3 If enquiries show that there is an insurer who is obliged to accept and does accept the obligation to handle the claim against the user of the vehicle concerned, even though the relevant liability may not be covered by the policy in question, then the claim should be pursued with such insurer.

4.4 If, however, enquiries disclose that there is no insurance covering the use of the vehicle concerned or if the insurer cannot be identified or the insurer asserts that it is under no obligation to handle the claim or if for any other reason it is clear that the insurer will not satisfy any judgment, the claim should be directed to MIB itself.

5   When proceedings are commenced or contemplated

5.1 As explained above, MIB does not have to wait for a judgment to be obtained before intervening. Claimants may apply to MIB before the commencement of proceedings. MIB will respond to any claim which complies with Clause 7 and must give a reasoned reply to any request for compensation in respect of the claim (see Clause 18) although normally a request for compensation will not be met until MIB is satisfied that it is properly based. Interim compensation payments are dealt with at paragraph 8 below.

5.2 It is important that wherever possible claims should be made using MIB's application form, fully completed and accompanied by documents supporting the claim, as soon as possible to avoid unnecessary delays. See Clause 7(1). Copies of the form can be obtained by downloading from this website or on request made by post, telephone, fax or the DX or on personal application to MIB's offices.

5.3 Where a claim is submitted to MIB, MIB will, with the claimant's agreement, deal with the claim on the basis of the pre-action Protocol set out in the Appendix. When it is decided to commence legal proceedings, contact should be made with MIB to ascertain if the case is one where it is appropriate for MIB to be joined as a defendant from the outset. In most cases this course will be beneficial, as it will simplify the task of notifying MIB of many of the legal processes as set out in Clauses 9 to 12, since once MIB is a defendant, the Court will advise the relevant events direct. However, this course can only be achieved with MIB's specific consent, using the form of words set out below in the pleadings and MIB will specify, in writing for the individual case, precisely what steps should be taken and which Clauses of the Agreement will be waived. Any Clause which is not waived must be complied with.

MIB joinder pleadings

1   The Second Defendant is a company limited by guarantee under the Companies Act. Pursuant to an Agreement with the Secretary of State

(dated 22nd December 1988 or 13th August 1999) (hereafter 'the Agreement') the Second Defendant provides compensation in certain circumstances to persons suffering injury or damage as a result of the negligence of uninsured motorists.

2   The Claimant has used all reasonable endeavours to ascertain the liability of an insurer for the First Defendant and at the time of commencement of these proceedings verily believes that the First Defendant is not insured.

3   The Claimant accepts that only if a final judgement is obtained against the First Defendant (which judgement is not satisfied in full within seven days from the date upon which the Claimant became entitled to enforce it) can the Second Defendant be required to satisfy the judgement and then only if the terms and conditions set out in the Agreement are satisfied. Until that time, any liability of the Second Defendant is only contingent.

4   To avoid the Second Defendant having later to apply separately to join itself in this action (which the Claimant must consent to in any event pursuant to Clause 14(b) of the Agreement*) the Claimant seeks to include the Second Defendant from the outset recognising fully the Second Defendant's position as reflected at 3 above and the rights of the Second Defendant fully to participate in the action to protect its position as a separate party to the action.

5   With the above in mind, the Claimant seeks a Declaration of the Second Defendant's contingent liability for damages to the Claimant in this action.

* This phrase is only relevant to the 1999 Agreement.

5.4   Unless MIB is joined to the action from the outset, the claimant must give MIB notice in writing that he has commenced legal proceedings. The notice, the completed application form (if appropriate) and all necessary documents must be received by MIB no later than 14 days after the date of commencement of proceedings. See Clause 9(1) and (2)(a). The date of commencement is determined in accordance with the definitions of 'relevant proceedings' and 'commencement' given in Clause 1.

5.5   This notice must have with it the following:

(a)   a copy of the document originating the proceedings, usually in England and Wales a Claim Form and in Scotland a Sheriff Court Writ or Court of Session Summons (see Clause 9(2)(b));

(b)   normally the Particulars of Claim endorsed on or served with the Claim Form or Writ (see Clause 9(2)(e), although this document may be served later in accordance with Clause 9(3) if that applies);

(c)   in any case the documents required by the relevant rules of procedure (see Clause 9(2)(f).

5.6   In addition, other items as mentioned in Clause 9(2), eg, correspondence with the Defendant (or Defender) or his representatives, need to be supplied where appropriate.

5.7 It is for the claimant to satisfy himself that the notice has in fact been received by MIB. Clause 8 applies to service of documents by post and fax. MIB prefer service by fax as it is almost instantaneous and can be confirmed quickly. However, whilst Clause 8 is specific as to the method of giving notice MIB will not automatically reject notice given by other means, provided the notice complies with the Agreement in all other respects. Nonetheless, claimants would be wise to comply with Clause 8, as doing so provides certainty that the appropriate notice has been received.

5.8 It should be noted that when MIB has been given notice of a claim, it may elect to require the claimant to bring proceedings and attempt to secure a judgment against the party whom MIB alleges to be wholly or partly responsible for the loss or damage or who may be contracted to indemnify the claimant. In such a case MIB must indemnify the claimant against the costs of such proceedings. Subject to that, however, MIB's obligation to satisfy the judgment in the action will only arise if the claimant commences the proceedings and takes all reasonable steps to obtain a judgment. See Clause 14(a).

6   Service of proceedings

6.1 If proceedings are commenced in England or Wales the claimant must inform MIB of the date of service (see Clause 10(1) and 10(2)).

6.2 If service of the Claim Form is effected by the Court, notice must be given within 7 days from the earliest of the dates listed in Clause 10(3)(a)(i) or (ii) or within 14 days from the date mentioned in Clause 10(3)(b) (the date of deemed service under the court's rules of procedure). Claimants are advised to take steps to ensure that the court or the defendant's legal representatives inform them of the date of service as soon as possible. Although a longer period is allowed than in other cases, service may be deemed to have occurred without a Claimant knowing of it until some time afterwards.

6.3 Where proceedings are served personally, notice must be given seven days from the date of personal service (see Clause 10(3)(a)(iii)).

6.4 In Scotland, proceedings are commenced at the date of service (see Clause 1) so notice should already have been given under Clause 9 and Clause 10 does not apply there.

7   After service and before judgment

7.1 Clauses 11 and 12 set out further notice requirements. However, the need to comply with these Clauses can be avoided by joining MIB to the legal action from the outset as a Defendant as explained above (Note 5.3). Where this is done, MIB will specifically waive reliance on these Clauses, in writing. If these Clauses are not waived in the individual case, they must be complied with.

7.2 Notice of the filing of a defence, of an amendment to the Statement or Particulars of Claim, and the setting down of the case for trial must be given not later than 7 days after the occurrence of such events and a copy of the document must be supplied (see Clause 11(1)).

7.3 MIB may request further information and documents to support the claim where it is not satisfied that the documents supplied with the application form are sufficient to enable it to assess its liability under the Agreement (see Clause 11(2)).

7.4 If the claimant intends to sign or apply for judgment he must give MIB notice of the fact before doing so. This notice must be given at least 35 days before the application is to be made or the date when judgment is to be signed (see Clause 12).

7.5 At no time must the claimant oppose MIB if it wishes to be joined as a party to proceedings and he must if requested consent to any application by MIB to be joined. Conflicts may arise between a Defendant and MIB which require MIB to become a Defendant or, in Scotland, a party Minuter if a defence is to be filed on its behalf (see Clause 14(b)).

8   Interim payments

In substantial cases, the claimant may wish to apply for an interim payment. MIB will consider such applications on a voluntary basis but otherwise the claimant has the right to apply to the court for an interim payment order which, if granted, will be met by MIB.

9   After judgment

9.1 MIB's basic obligation normally arises if a judgment is not satisfied within 7 days after the claimant has become entitled to enforce it (see Clause 1). However, that judgment may in certain circumstances be set aside and with it MIB's obligation to satisfy it. Sometimes MIB wishes to apply to set aside a judgment either wholly or partially. If MIB decides not to satisfy a judgment it will notify the claimant as soon as possible. Where a judgment is subsequently set aside, MIB will require the claimant to repay any sum previously paid by MIB to discharge its obligation under the Agreement (see Clause 15(b)).

9.2 MIB is not obliged to satisfy a judgment unless the claimant has in return assigned the benefit to MIB or its nominee (see Clause 15(a)). If such assignment is effected and if the subject matter of the judgment includes claims in respect of which MIB is not obliged to meet any judgment and if MIB effects any recovery on the judgment, the sum recovered will be divided between MIB and the claimant in proportion to the liabilities which were and which were not covered by MIB's obligation (see Clause 21).

10   Permissible deductions from payments by MIB

10.1 Claims for loss and damage for which the claimant has been compensated or indemnified, eg, under a contract of insurance or under the Policyholders Protection Act 1975, and which has not been taken into account in the judgment, may be deducted from the sum paid in settlement of MIB's obligation (see Clause 17).

10.2 If there is a likelihood that the claimant will receive payment from such a source after the judgment has been satisfied by MIB, MIB will require him to undertake to repay any sum which duplicates the compensation assessed by the court (see Clause 15(b)).

11   Untraced drivers

11.1 Where the owner or driver of a vehicle cannot be identified application may be made to MIB under the relevant Untraced Drivers Agreement. This provides, subject to specified conditions, for the payment of compensation for personal injury. It does not provide for compensation in respect of damage to property.

11.2 In those cases where it is unclear whether the owner or driver of a vehicle has been correctly identified it is sensible for the claimant to register a claim under both this Agreement and the Untraced Drivers Agreement following which MIB will advise which Agreement will, in its view, apply in the circumstances of the particular case.

UNINSURED – APPLICATION FORM NOTES

These notes apply specifically to England, Wales and Scotland. However, they are also broadly applicable to Northern Ireland.

These notes appear in question and answer format and deal with those questions that are most often raised by claimants.

The notes relate specifically to the latest Agreement (13 August 1999) but do not replace or modify the Agreement and claimants are recommended to read the text of the Agreement under which they are submitting a claim.

Notes for the assistance of claimants

Q
What is the 'Uninsured Drivers' Agreement?

A
This is an Agreement between the Secretary of State for the Environment, Transport and the Regions and MIB which sets out the circumstances under which claims will be paid. Whilst the Agreement requires that judgement be obtained in a Civil Court against the uninsured motorist, MIB will, wherever possible, pay compensation by agreement as opposed to demanding that a judgement be obtained first. The text of the Agreement can be ordered from the Stationery Office website, or alternatively, the printed version can be obtained from the Stationery Office or large booksellers for a small charge.

Q
When should I claim on MIB?

A
As soon as it becomes clear that the motorist who has caused the injury or damage is uninsured, MIB expects that a claimant will have made common sense enquiries to identify an insurer, which enquiries will include but not necessarily be limited to:

Contacting the motorist.

Enquiring of the Driver and Vehicle Licensing Authority in Swansea as to the identity of the registered keeper of the vehicle. (The registered keeper of the vehicle is more likely to have insurance information than the driver.)

Searching any computer database that may be available for the purpose.

Making a formal complaint to the police under section 154 of the Road Traffic Act 1988. (Section 154 makes it an offence for a person against whom a claim is made to withhold details of insurance.)

Q
What information and/or documents should I provide when returning this form?

A
Copies of all correspondence with the motorist, the owner/registered keeper of the vehicle, the motorist's employer or anyone acting on their behalf, including any insurer regardless of whether the insurer denies issuing cover. Your claim will have to be proved, so much time can be saved by enclosing documents supporting your claim. For example, estimates for any repair required, or if you have lost earnings, a letter from your employers confirming exactly what has been lost. It is essential that, if you were driving a motor vehicle, you enclose evidence that you were insured at the time, as the Agreement excludes compensation for damage to property if the vehicle is uninsured. It is very important that as much information as possible is given, since if information is withheld unreasonably, any court which hears the case subsequently has the power to impose financial penalties.

Q
What will happen after I return this form?

A
MIB will confirm receipt as soon as possible and explain what action is being taken, which action will vary depending on the case and the information you have been able to supply. However, as well as investigating the amount of your claim, we must try and contact the uninsured motorist to obtain his account of the accident as well as his permission to intervene.

Q
Why do you need the permission of the uninsured motorist to deal with my claim?

A
Even uninsured motorists have the right in law to deal with their own affairs, and the Agreement does not permit us to ignore his rights. However, if the uninsured motorist does not co-operate, we will tell you what options appear to be available to progress your claim.

Q
What if the motorist cannot be identified?

A
If your claim is for damage to property, then unfortunately we will be unable to help you, as there is no possibility of your obtaining a judgment against the person responsible. However, if you have been injured, you will be able to submit a claim for that injury (but not damage to property) under the 'Untraced Drivers' Agreement, which provides for victims of 'hit and run' accidents.

Q	**A**
How long will my claim take?	This is difficult to predict as many different factors are involved:

If your claim is limited to property damage or minor injury it should be resolved in 4 or 5 months, or less.

If, on the other hand, your claim involves contested liability, evidentiary difficulties, or serious injury it may require the police report to be obtained, which can take some time, especially if its release is delayed by criminal prosecutions.

Injury claims can also be delayed if it is difficult for your doctors to agree on the effects, and you may be advised to wait until you have recovered fully, before agreeing any compensation.

MIB will make every effort to reach a decision on responsibility for the accident within three months and to keep you informed. Where there seems to be the prospect of a long delay, MIB will consider an interim payment.

Q	**A**
Will my claim be paid in full?	Responsibility for the accident has to be agreed, or decided by a Court, on the evidence, and your claim may be reduced by a proportion, or possibly rejected if the evidence is that you were wholly or partly responsible.

Where MIB accepts a claim is one for payment, property damage claims (which includes claims for losses arising from the damage to property, as may be allowed by a court) will have an excess of £300 deducted. If the accident occurred before 1 October 1999, the excess applicable (under the previous 'Uninsured Drivers' Agreement) will be £175.

Injury claims, including loss of earnings, are subject to a legal obligation on MIB to refund to the Department of Social Security certain benefits that you have been paid as a result of the accident, and to deduct that amount from your claim for loss of earnings. You are advised by the DSS as to the amount MIB has to pay and if you disagree, you have a right of appeal to the DSS.

Q	A
What can I do if I think I have grounds for complaint?	MIB deals with all claims in accordance with service standards, and seeks to provide a reasoned response wherever necessary. Nonetheless, if you are dissatisfied, this is what you should do:

Contact your solicitors or representative and ask him to resolve the problem by telephone.

If you are not represented, telephone MIB (or the agent who is handling the matter on behalf of MIB) and speak to the person handling the claim. If you are not satisfied, write 'for the attention of the Claims Manager'. In the event you feel that the complaint has not been resolved, write to the Technical Director, MIB, Linford Wood House, 6–12 Capital Drive, Linford Wood, Milton Keynes, MK14 6XT, marking the envelope 'Private and Confidential'.

The Chief Executive of MIB is always prepared to review decisions on complaints. Should you wish to do so, please write to him at the same address.

In the event that your problem involves a matter of principle, which may be of public interest and you consider that it has not been dealt with adequately under the above procedure, it is open to you to write to the Minister for Roads and Traffic at the Department of the Environment, Transport and the Regions, Great Minster House, 76 Marsham Street, London, SWIP 4DR. The Minister will normally require to be satisfied that the above procedure has been followed before he will intervene.

Important Note: A problem arising from the interpretation of the Agreement can only be resolved by reference to the court, unless the Agreement specifically empowers the Minister to intervene.

THE REVISED NOTES FOR GUIDANCE 2002

NOTES FOR THE GUIDANCE OF VICTIMS OF
ROAD TRAFFIC ACCIDENTS

The following notes are for the guidance of anyone who may have a claim on the Motor Insurers' Bureau under this Agreement and their legal advisers. They are not part of the Agreement, their purpose being to deal in ordinary language with the situations which most readily occur. They are not in any way a substitute for reading and applying the terms of this or any other relevant Agreement.

At the request of the Secretary of State, these notes have been revised with effect from 15th April 2002 and in their revised form have been agreed and approved by MIB, the Law Society of England and Wales, the Law Society of Scotland, the Motor Accident Solicitors Society and the Association of Personal Injury Lawyers. Any application made under the Agreement after this date (unless proceedings have already been issued) will be handled by MIB in accordance with these notes.

Where proceedings have been issued in Scotland, for the words 'Claimant' and 'Defendant' there shall be substituted in these Notes where appropriate the words 'Pursuer' and 'Defender' respectively.

Enquiries, requests for application forms and general correspondence in connection with the Agreement should be addressed to:

Motor Insurers' Bureau
Linford Wood House
6–12 Capital Drive
MILTON KEYNES
MK14 6XT

Tel: 01908 830001
Fax: 01908 671681
DX: 142620 Milton Keynes 10

1 Introduction – MIB's role and application of the Agreement

1.1 The role of MIB under this Agreement is to provide a safety net for innocent victims of drivers who have been identified but are uninsured. MIB's funds for this purpose are obtained from levies charged upon insurers and so come from the premiums which are charged by those insurers to members of the public.

1.2   MIB has entered into a series of Agreements with the Secretary of State and his predecessors in office. Under each Agreement MIB undertakes obligations to pay defined compensation in specific circumstances. There are two sets of Agreements, one relating to victims of uninsured drivers (the Uninsured Drivers Agreements) and the other concerned with victims of hit and run or otherwise untraceable drivers (the Untraced Drivers Agreements). These Notes are addressed specifically to the procedures required to take advantage of the rights granted by the Uninsured Drivers Agreements. However, it is not always certain which of the Agreements applies. For guidance in such cases please see the note on Untraced Drivers at paragraph 11 below.

1.3   In order to determine which of the Uninsured Drivers Agreements is applicable to a particular victim's claim, regard must be had to the date of the relevant accident. This Agreement only applies in respect of claims arising on or after 1st October 1999. Claims arising earlier than that are covered by the following Agreements:

1.3.1   Claims arising in respect of an incident occurring between 1st July 1946 and 28th February 1971 are governed by the Agreement between the Minister of Transport and the Bureau dated 17th June 1946.

1.3.2   Claims arising in respect of an incident occurring between 1st March 1971 and 30th November 1972 are governed by the Agreement between the Secretary of State for the Environment and the Bureau dated 1st February 1971.

1.3.3   Claims arising in respect of an incident occurring between 1st December 1972 and 30th December 1988 are governed by the Agreement between the Secretary of State and the Bureau dated 22nd November 1972.

1.3.4   Claims arising in respect of an incident occurring between 31st December 1988 and 30th September 1999 are governed by the Agreement between the Secretary of State and the Bureau dated 21st December 1988.

2   MIB's obligation

2.1   MIB's basic obligation (see Clause 5) is to satisfy judgments which fall within the terms of this Agreement and which, because the Defendant to the proceedings is not insured, are not satisfied.

2.2   This obligation is, however, not absolute. It is subject to certain exceptions where MIB has no liability (see Clause 6), there are a number of pre-conditions which the claimant must comply with (see Clauses 7 to 15) and there are some limitations on MIB's liability (see Clauses 16 and 17).

2.3 **Nothing in the Agreement is intended to vary the limitation rules applying to claimants not of full age or capacity. Limitation for personal injury remains three years from the date of full age or capacity.**

2.4 MIB does not have to wait for a judgment to be given; it can become party to the proceedings or negotiate and settle the claim if it wishes to do so.

3 Claims which MIB is not obliged to satisfy

MIB is not liable under the Agreement in the case of the following types of claim.

3.1 A claim made in respect of an unsatisfied judgment which does not concern a liability against which Part VI of the Road Traffic Act 1988 requires a vehicle user to insure (see section 145 of the Act). An example would be a case where the accident did not occur in a place specified in the Act. See the definitions of 'unsatisfied judgment' and 'relevant liability' in Clause 1.

3.2 A claim in respect of loss or damage caused by the use of a vehicle owned by or in the possession of the Crown (that is the Civil Service, the armed forces and so on) to which Part VI does not apply. If the responsibility for motor insurance has been undertaken by someone else or the vehicle is in fact insured, this exception does not apply. See Clause 6(1)(a).

3.3 A claim made against any person who is not required to insure by virtue of section 144 of the Road Traffic Act 1988. See Clause 6(1)(b).

3.4 A claim (commonly called subrogated) made in the name of a person suffering damage or injury but which is in fact wholly or partly for the benefit of another who has indemnified, or is liable to indemnify that person. See Clause 6(1)(c).

It is not the intention of this Clause to exclude claims for the gratuitous provision of care, travel expenses by family members or friends, or miscellaneous expenses incurred on behalf of the Claimant, where the Claimant is entitled to include such claims in his claim for damages.

3.5 A claim in respect of damage to a motor vehicle or losses arising from such damage where the use of the damaged vehicle was itself not covered by a contract of insurance as required by law. See Clause 6(1)(d).

3.6 A claim made by a passenger in a vehicle where the loss or damage has been caused by the user of that vehicle if:

3.6.1 the use of the vehicle was not covered by a contract of insurance; and

3.6.2 the claimant knew or could be taken to have known that the vehicle was being used without insurance, had been stolen or unlawfully taken or was being used in connection with crime.

See Clause 6(1)(e), (2), (3) and (4).

For an interpretation of 'knew or ought to have known' refer to the House of Lords judgment in *White v White* of 1st March 2001.

3.7 A claim in respect of property damage amounting to £300 or less, £300 being the 'specified excess'. See Clause 16(2).

3.8 Where the claim is for property damage, the first £300 of the loss and so much of it as exceeds £250,000. See Clause 16(3) and (4).

4 Procedure after the accident and before proceedings

4.1 The claimant must take reasonable steps to establish whether there is in fact any insurance covering the use of the vehicle which caused the injury or damage. First, a claimant has statutory rights under section 154 of the Road Traffic Act 1988 to obtain relevant particulars which he must take steps to exercise even if that involves incurring expense and MIB will insist that he does so. See Clause 13(a).

MIB accept that if the MIB application form is sufficiently completed and signed by the Claimant, the Claimant will have complied with this Clause of the Agreement.

4.2 Other steps will include the following:

4.2.1 The exchange of names, addresses and insurance particulars between those involved either at the scene of the accident or afterwards.

4.2.2 Corresponding with the owner or driver of the vehicle or his representatives. He will be obliged under the terms of his motor policy to inform his insurers and a letter of claim addressed to him will commonly be passed to the insurers who may reply on his behalf. See Clause 9(2)(d).

4.2.3 Where only the vehicle's number is known, enquiry of the Driver and Vehicle Licensing Agency at Swansea SA99 1BP as to the registered keeper of the vehicle is desirable so that through him the identity of the owner or driver can be established or confirmed.

4.2.4 Enquiries of the police (see Clause 13(b) *and Note 4.1 above*).

4.3 If enquiries show that there is an insurer who is obliged to accept and does accept the obligation to handle the claim against the user of the vehicle concerned, even though the relevant liability may not be covered by the policy in question, then the claim should be pursued with such insurer.

4.4 If, however, enquiries disclose that there is no insurance covering the use of the vehicle concerned or if the insurer cannot be identified or the insurer asserts that it is under no obligation to handle the claim or if for any other reason it is clear that the insurer will not satisfy any judgment, the claim should be directed to MIB itself.

5   When proceedings are commenced or contemplated

5.1   As explained above, MIB does not have to wait for a judgment to be obtained before intervening. Claimants may apply to MIB before the commencement of proceedings. MIB will respond to any claim which complies with Clause 7 and must give a reasoned reply to any request for compensation in respect of the claim (see Clause 18) although normally a request for compensation will not be met until MIB is satisfied that it is properly based. Interim compensation payments are dealt with at paragraph 8 below.

Application forms are available from MIB's office or their website: www.mib.org.uk.

Where a claim is made by the Claimant in person, who has not received legal advice, then if the claim is first made within 14 days prior to expiry of the limitation period, MIB will require the completed application form within 21 days after the issue of proceedings.

5.2   It is important that wherever possible claims should be made using MIB's application form, fully completed and accompanied by documents supporting the claim, as soon as possible to avoid unnecessary delays. See Clause 7(1). Copies of the form can be obtained on request made by post, telephone, fax or the DX or on personal application to MIB's offices.

5.3   The claimant must give MIB notice *in writing* that he has commenced legal proceedings. The notice, the completed application form (if appropriate) and all necessary documents must be received by MIB no later than 14 days after the date of commencement of proceedings. See Clause 9(1) and (2)(a). The date of commencement is determined in accordance with the definitions of 'relevant proceedings' and 'commencement' given in Clause 1.

When it is decided to commence legal proceedings, MIB should be joined as a defendant (unless there is good reason not to do so). Once MIB is a defendant, the Court will advise the relevant events direct and Clauses 9(3), 11 and 12 will no longer apply.

The form of words set out below should be used for the joinder of MIB as second defendant:

1   **The Second Defendant is a Company limited by guarantee under the Companies Act. Pursuant to an Agreement with the Secretary of State for the Environment, Transport and the Regions dated 13th August 1999, the Second Defendant provides compensation in certain circumstances to persons suffering injury or damage as a result of the negligence of uninsured motorists.**

2   **The Claimant has used all reasonable endeavours to ascertain the liability of an insurer for the First Defendant and at the time of the commencement of these proceedings verily believes that the First Defendant is not insured.**

3   The Claimant accepts that only if a final judgment is obtained against the First Defendant (which judgment is not satisfied in full within seven days from the date upon which the Claimant became entitled to enforce it) can the Second Defendant be required to satisfy the judgement and then only if the terms and conditions set out in the Agreement are satisfied. Until that time, any liability of the Second Defendant is only contingent.

4   To avoid the Second Defendant having later to apply to join itself to this action (which the Claimant must consent to in any event, pursuant to Clause 14(b) of the Agreement) the Claimant seeks to include the Second Defendant from the outset recognising fully the Second Defendant's position as reflected in 3 above and the rights of the Second Defendant fully to participate in the action to protect its position as a separate party to the action.

5   With the above in mind, the Claimant seeks a declaration of the Second Defendant's contingent liability to satisfy the claimant's judgment against the First Defendant.

5.4   This notice must have with it the following:

5.4.1   a copy of the document originating the proceedings, usually in England and Wales a Claim Form and in Scotland a Sheriff Court Writ or Court of Session Summons (see Clause 9(2)(b));

5.4.2   normally the Particulars of Claim endorsed on or served with the Claim Form or Writ (see Clause 9(2)(e), although this document may be served later in accordance with Clause 9(3) if that applies);

5.4.3   in any case the documents required by the relevant rules of procedure (see Clause 9(2)(f).

Provided that the documents referred to above are forwarded to MIB, it is not necessary to enclose the Response Pack or the Notice of Issue.

5.5   In addition, other items as mentioned in Clause 9(2), eg, correspondence with the Defendant (or Defender) or his representatives, need to be supplied where appropriate.

5.6   It is for the claimant to satisfy himself that the notice has in fact been received by MIB.

However, where the Claimant proves that service by DX, First Class Post, Personal Service or any other form of service allowed by the Civil Procedure Rules, was effected, MIB will accept that such notice has been served in the same circumstances in which a party to litigation would be obliged to accept that he had been validly served by such means.

5.7   It should be noted that when MIB has been given notice of a claim, it may elect to require the claimant to bring proceedings and attempt to secure a judgment against the party whom MIB alleges to be wholly or partly responsible for the loss or damage or who may be contracted to indemnify the claimant. In such a case MIB must indemnify the claimant against the costs of such proceedings. Subject to that, however, MIB's obligation to satisfy the judgment in the action will only arise if the claimant commences the proceedings and takes all reasonable steps to obtain a judgment. See Clause 14(a).

6 Service of proceedings

6.1 If proceedings are commenced in England or Wales the claimant *must* inform MIB of the date of service (see Clause 10(1) and (2)).

6.2 If service of the Claim Form is effected by the Court, notice **should** be given within 7 days from the earliest of the dates listed in Clause 10(3)(a)(i) or (ii) or within 14 days from the date mentioned in Clause 10(3)(b) (the date of deemed service under the court's rules of procedure). Claimants are advised to take steps to ensure that the court or the defendant's legal representatives inform them of the date of service as soon as possible. Although a longer period is allowed than in other cases, service may be deemed to have occurred without a Claimant knowing of it until some time afterwards.

6.3 Where proceedings are served personally, notice **should** be given seven days from the date of personal service (Clause 10(3)(a)(iii)).

6.4 However, by concession MIB will accept the notice referred to in Note 6.1 above if it is received by MIB within 14 days from the dates referred to in Notes 6.2 and 6.3.

6.5 In Scotland, proceedings are commenced at the date of service (see Clause 1) so notice should already have been given under Clause 9 and Clause 10 does not apply there.

7 After service and before judgment

See Note 5.3 above.

7.1 Notice of the filing of a defence, of an amendment to the Statement or Particulars of Claim, and the setting down of the case for trial should be given not later than seven days after the occurrence of such events and a copy of the document **must** be supplied (Clause 11(1)).

7.2 However, by concession MIB will accept the notice referred to in note 7.1 above if it is received by MIB within 14 days after the proven date on which it was received by the claimant.

7.3 MIB may request further information and documents to support the claim where it is not satisfied that the documents supplied with the application form are sufficient to enable it to assess its liability under the Agreement (see Clause 11(2)).

7.4 If the claimant intends to sign or apply for judgment he must give MIB notice of the fact before doing so. This notice must be given at least 35 days before the application is to be made or the date when judgment is to be signed (see Clause 12).

The 35 days notice does not apply where the court enters judgment of its own motion.

7.5 At no time must the claimant oppose MIB if it wishes to be joined as a party to proceedings and he must if requested consent to any application by MIB to be joined. Conflicts may arise between a Defendant and MIB which require MIB to become a Defendant or, in Scotland, a party Minuter if a defence is to be filed on its behalf (see Clause 14(b)).

8 Interim payments

In substantial cases, the claimant may wish to apply for an interim payment. MIB will consider such applications on a voluntary basis but otherwise the claimant has the right to apply to the court for an interim payment order which, if granted, will be met by MIB.

9 After judgment

9.1 MIB's basic obligation normally arises if a judgment is not satisfied within seven days after the claimant has become entitled to enforce it (see Clause 1). However, that judgment may in certain circumstances be set aside and with it MIB's obligation to satisfy it. Sometimes MIB wishes to apply to set aside a judgment either wholly or partially. If MIB decides not to satisfy a judgment it will notify the claimant as soon as possible. Where a judgment is subsequently set aside, MIB will require the claimant to repay any sum previously paid by MIB to discharge its obligation under the Agreement (see Clause 15(b)).

9.2 MIB is not obliged to satisfy a judgment unless the claimant has in return assigned the benefit to MIB or its nominee (see Clause 15(a)). If such assignment is effected and if the subject matter of the judgment includes claims in respect of which MIB is not obliged to meet any judgment and if MIB effects any recovery on the judgment, the sum recovered will be divided between MIB and the claimant in proportion to the liabilities which were and which were not covered by MIB's obligation (see Clause 21).

10 Permissible deductions from payments by MIB

10.1 Claims for loss and damage for which the claimant has been compensated or indemnified, eg, under a contract of insurance or under the Policyholders Protection Act 1975, and which has not been taken into account in the judgment, may be deducted from the sum paid in settlement of MIB's obligation (see Clause 17).

10.2 If there is a likelihood that the claimant will receive payment from such a source after the judgment has been satisfied by MIB, MIB will require him to undertake to repay any sum which duplicates the compensation assessed by the court (see Clause 15(b)).

11 Untraced drivers

11.1 Where the owner or driver of a vehicle cannot be identified application may be made to MIB under the relevant Untraced Drivers Agreement. This provides, subject to specified conditions, for the payment of compensation for personal **injury**. It *does not* provide for compensation in respect of damage to property.

11.2 In those cases where it is unclear whether the owner or driver of a vehicle has been correctly identified it is sensible for the claimant to register a claim under both this Agreement and the Untraced Drivers Agreement following which MIB will advise which Agreement will, in its view, apply in the circumstances of the particular case.

© *Motor Insurers' Bureau 2002*

THE UNINSURED DRIVERS AGREEMENT 1988

21st December 1988

DEPARTMENT OF TRANSPORT

MOTOR INSURERS' BUREAU (COMPENSATION OF VICTIMS OF UNINSURED DRIVERS)

Text of an Agreement dated 21st December 1988 between the Secretary of State for Transport and the Motor Insurers' Bureau together with some notes on its scope and purpose

In accordance with the Agreement made on 31 December 1945 between the Minister of War Transport and insurers transacting compulsory motor vehicle insurance business in Great Britain (published by the Stationery Office under the title 'Motor Vehicle Insurance Fund') a corporation called the 'Motor Insurers' Bureau' entered into an agreement on 17 June 1946 to the principle recommended in July 1937 by the Departmental Committee under Sir Felix Cassel (Cmnd 5528), to secure compensation to third party victims of road accidents in cases where, notwithstanding the provisions of the Road Traffic Acts relating to compulsory insurance, the victim is deprived of compensation by the absence of insurance, or of effective insurance.

That Agreement was replaced by an Agreement which operated in respect of accidents occurring on or after 1 March 1971 which in turn was replaced by a new Agreement which operated in respect of accidents occurring on or after 1 December 1972. The Agreement of 1972 has now been replaced by a new Agreement which operates in respect of accidents occurring on or after 31 December 1988.

The text of the new Agreement is as follows:

MEMORANDUM OF AGREEMENT made the 21st day of December 1988 between the Secretary of State for Transport and the Motor Insurers' Bureau, whose registered office is at New Garden House, 78 Hatton Garden, London ECIN 8JQ (hereinafter referred to as 'MIB').

SUPPLEMENTAL to an Agreement (hereinafter called 'the Principal Agreement') made the 31st day of December 1945 between the Minister of War Transport and the insurers transacting compulsory motor insurance business in Great Britain by or on behalf of whom the said Agreement was signed and in pursuance of paragraph 1 of which MIB was incorporated.

IT IS HEREBY AGREED AS FOLLOWS:

DEFINITIONS

1   In this Agreement:

- 'contract of insurance' means a policy of insurance or a security;

- 'insurer' includes the giver of a security;

- 'relevant liability' means a liability in respect of which a policy of insurance must insure a person in order to comply with Part VI of the Road Traffic Act 1972, and references to the Road Traffic Act 1972 are references to that Act as amended by the Motor Vehicles (Compulsory Insurance) Regulations 1987 (No 2171).

SATISFACTION OF CLAIMS BY MIB

2.1   If judgment in respect of any relevant liability is obtained against any person or persons in any Court in Great Britain whether or not such a person or persons be in fact covered by a contract of insurance and any such judgment is not satisfied in full within seven days from the date upon which the person or persons in whose favour the judgment was given became entitled to enforce it then MIB will, subject to the provisions of paragraphs (2), (3) and (4) below and to Clauses 4, 5 and 6 hereof, pay or satisfy or cause to be paid or satisfied to or to the satisfaction of the person or persons in whose favour the judgment was given any sum payable or remaining payable thereunder in respect of the relevant liability including any sum awarded by the Court in respect of interest on that sum and any taxed costs or any costs awarded by the Court without taxation (or such proportion thereof as is attributable to the relevant liability) whatever may be the cause of the failure of the judgment debtor to satisfy the judgment.

2.2   Subject to paragraphs (3) and (4) below and to Clauses 4, 5 and 6 hereof, MIB shall incur liability under paragraph (1) above in respect of any sum awarded under such a judgment in respect of property damage not exceeding £250,000 or in respect of the first £250,000 of any sum so awarded exceeding that amount.

2.3   Where a person in whose favour a judgment in respect of relevant liability which includes liability in respect of damage to property has been given, has received or is entitled to receive in consequence of a claim he has made, compensation from any source in respect of that damage, MIB may deduct from the sum payable or remaining payable under paragraph (1) above an amount equal to the amount of that compensation in addition to the deduction of £175 by virtue of paragraph (4) below. The reference to compensation includes compensation under insurance arrangements.

2.4 MIB shall not incur liability under paragraph (1) above in respect of any amount payable or remaining payable under the judgment in respect of property damage liability where the total of amounts so payable or remaining payable is £175 or less, or, where the total of such amounts is more than £175, in respect of the first £175 of such total.

PERIOD OF AGREEMENT

3.1 This Agreement shall be determinable by the Secretary of State at any time or by MIB on 12 months' notice without prejudice to the continued operation of the Agreement in respect of accidents occurring before the date of termination.

RECOVERIES

4.1 Nothing in this Agreement shall prevent insurers from providing by conditions in their contracts of insurance that all sums paid by them or by MIB by virtue of the Principal Agreement or this Agreement in or towards the discharge of the liability of their insured shall be recoverable by them or by MIB from the insured or from any other person.

CONDITIONS PRECEDENT TO MIB'S LIABILITY

5.1 MIB shall not incur any liability under Clause 2 of this Agreement unless –

(a) notice in writing of the bringing of the proceedings is given within seven days after the commencement of the proceedings:

    (i) to MIB in the case of proceedings in respect of a relevant liability which is either not covered by a contract of insurance or covered by a contract of insurance with an insurer whose identity cannot be ascertained, or

    (ii) to the insurer in the case of proceedings in respect of a relevant liability which is covered by a contract of insurance with an insurer whose identity can be ascertained;

such notice shall be accompanied by a copy of the writ, summons or other document initiating the proceedings;

(b) the person bringing the proceedings furnishes to MIB –

    (i) such information (in such form as MIB may specify) in relation thereto as MIB may reasonably require, and

    (ii) such information (in such form as MIB may specify) as to any insurance covering any damage to property to which the claim or proceedings relate and any claim made in respect of that damage under the insurance or otherwise and any report which may have been made or notification which may have been given to any person in respect of that damage or the use of the vehicle giving rise thereto, as MIB may reasonably require;

(c) the person bringing the proceedings has demanded the information and, where appropriate, the particulars specified in section 151 of the Road Traffic Act 1972 in accordance with that section or, if so required by MIB, has authorised MIB to do so on his behalf;

(d) if so required by MIB and subject to full indemnity from MIB as to costs the person bringing the proceedings has taken all reasonable steps to obtain judgment against all the persons liable in respect of the injury or death or damage to property and, in the event of any such person being a servant or agent, against his principal; and

(e) the judgment referred to in Clause 2 of this Agreement and any judgment referred to in paragraph (d) of this Clause which has been obtained (whether or not either judgment includes an amount in respect of a liability other than a relevant liability) and any order for costs are assigned to MIB or their nominee.

5.2   In the event of any dispute as to the reasonableness of a requirement by MIB for the supply of information or that any particular step should be taken to obtain judgment against other persons it may be referred to the Secretary of State whose decision shall be final.

5.3   Where a judgment which includes an amount in respect of a liability other than a relevant liability has been assigned to MIB or their nominee in pursuance of paragraph (1)(e) of this Clause MIB shall apportion any monies received in pursuance of the judgment according to the proportion which the damages in respect of the relevant liability bear to the damages in respect of the other liabilities and shall account to the person in whose favour the judgment was given in respect of such monies received properly apportionable to the other liabilities. Where an order for costs in respect of such a judgment has been so assigned monies received pursuant to the order shall be dealt with in the same manner.

EXCEPTIONS

6.1   MIB shall not incur any liability under Clause 2 of this Agreement in a case where:

(a) the claim arises out of the use of a vehicle owned by or in the possession of the Crown, except where any other person has undertaken responsibility for the existence of a contract of insurance under Part IV of the Road Traffic Act 1972 (whether or not the person or persons liable be in fact covered by a contract of insurance) or where the liability is in fact covered by a contract of insurance;

(b)   the claim arises out of the use of a vehicle the use of which is required to be covered by a contract of insurance by virtue of section 144 of the Road Traffic Act 1972, unless the use is in fact covered by such a contract:

(c)   the claim is in respect of a judgment or any part thereof which has been obtained by virtue of the exercise of a right of subrogation by any person;

(d)   the claim is in respect of damage to property which consists of damage to a motor vehicle or losses arising therefrom if at the time of the use giving rise to the damage to the motor vehicle there was not in force in relation to the use of that vehicle when the damage to it was sustained such a policy of insurance as is required by Part VI of the Road Traffic Act 1972 and the person or persons claiming in respect of the loss or damage either knew or ought to have known that that was the case;

(e)   at the time of the use which gave rise to the liability the person suffering death or bodily injury or damage to property was allowing himself to be carried in or upon the vehicle and either before the commencement of his journey in the vehicle or after such commencement if he could reasonably be expected to have alighted from the vehicle he –

(i)   knew or ought to have known that the vehicle had been stolen or unlawfully taken, or

(ii)   knew or ought to have known that the vehicle was being used without there being in force in relation to its use such a contract of insurance as would comply with Part VI of the Road Traffic Act 1972.

6.2   The exception specific in sub-paragraph (1)(e) of this Clause shall apply only in a case where the judgment in respect of which the claim against MIB is made was obtained in respect of a relevant liability incurred by the owner or a person using the vehicle in which the person who suffered death or bodily injury or sustained damage to property was being carried.

6.3   For the purposes of these exceptions –

(a)   a vehicle which has been unlawfully removed from the possession of the Crown shall be taken to continue in that possession whilst it is kept so removed;

(b)   references to a person being carried in a vehicle include references to his being carried in or upon or entering or getting onto or alighting from the vehicle; and

(c)   'owner' in relation to a vehicle which is the subject of a hiring agreement or a hire-purchase agreement, means the person in possession of the vehicle under that agreement.

AGENTS

7.1 Nothing in this Agreement shall prevent MIB performing their obligations under this Agreement by agents.

OPERATION

8.1 This Agreement shall come into operation on the 31st day of December 1988 in relation to accidents occurring on or after that date. The Agreement made on 22nd November 1972 between the Secretary of State and MIB shall cease and determine except in relation to claims arising out of accidents occurring before the 31st day of December 1988.

IN WITNESS whereof the Secretary of State has caused his Corporate Seal to be hereto affixed and the Motor Insurers' Bureau has caused their Common Seal to be hereto affixed the day and year first above written.

THE CORPORATE SEAL of the Secretary of State was hereunto affixed in the presence of DH Workskett.

An Assistant Secretary in the Department of Transport duly authorised in that behalf.

The COMMON SEAL of the Motor Insurers'
Bureau was hereunto affixed in the presence of
TA Kent Members of
A Kilpatrick The Council
JL West Secretary

THE UNINSURED DRIVERS AGREEMENT 1988
NOTES FOR GUIDANCE

The following notes are for the guidance of those who may have a claim on the Motor Insurers' Bureau under the Agreement, and of their legal advisers, but they must not be taken as rendering unnecessary a careful study of the Agreement itself. Communications on any matter connected with the Agreement should be addressed to Motor Insurers' Bureau whose address is 152 Silbury Boulevard, Central Milton Keynes MK9 1NB.

On the date of coming into force of the Road Traffic Act 1988 references to the provisions of the Road Traffic Act 1972 are by virtue of section 2(4) of the Road Traffic (Consequential Provisions) Act 1988 to be read as reference to the corresponding provisions of the Road Traffic Act 1988.

In order to up-date the Notes to the Agreement to reflect recent developments, an appendix has been added to the notes as published originally.

1 The Agreement, which operates from 31st December 1988 supersedes earlier Agreements made on 17 June 1946 (which was operative from 1 July 1946), on 1 February 1971 (which was operative from 1 March 1971) and on 22 November 1972 (which was operative from 1 December 1972) in relation to claims arising out of accidents occurring on or after that date.

2 If damages are awarded by a Court in respect of death or personal injury or damage to property arising out of the use of motor vehicle on a road in circumstances where the liability is one which was, at the time the accident occurred, required to be covered by insurance and such damages, or any part of them, remain unpaid seven days after the judgment becomes enforceable, the Bureau will, subject to the limit specified in Clause 2(2), which corresponds with the limited insurance requirement in section 145(4)(b) of the Road Traffic Act, and the exceptions in paragraphs (3) and (4) of Clause 2 and Clause 6 of the Agreement, pay the unrecovered amount (including any interest awarded by the Court and costs) to the person in whose favour the judgment has been given against an assignment of the judgment debt. This applies whether the judgment debtor is a British resident or a foreign visitor.

3 Clause 1 defines 'relevant liability' as a liability in respect of which a policy of insurance must insure a person in order to comply with Part VI of the Road Traffic Act 1972, which includes liability in respect of property damage caused by, or arising out of, the use of the motor vehicle on a road in Great Britain. This provision gives effect to Article 1.1 of Council Directive (84/5/EEC) of 30 December 1983 on the approximation of the laws of Member States relating to insurance against civil liability in respect of the use of motor vehicles (OJ No L8, 11.1.84, p17). In the context of the Directive 'damage to property' means damage to material property. Accordingly in this Agreement the reference to damage to property is understood in that sense. With regard to liability in respect of such damage which is covered by the Agreement, MIB would expect to meet the consequential loss elements of a claim flowing from damage to the claimant's material property which a Court would allow. It must be emphasised that MIB's obligation does not extend to those liabilities not required to be covered by the policy under section 145 of the Road Traffic Act 1972.

4 Nothing in the Agreement affects the position at law of the parties to an action for damages arising out of the driving of a motor vehicle. The Bureau's liability under the Agreement can only arise when the plaintiff has successfully established his case against the person or persons liable in the usual manner and judgment has been given in his favour. There is, of course, nothing to exclude the acceptance of compensation by the plaintiff under a settlement of his claim negotiated between the plaintiff and the alleged person liable or the Bureau.

5 The purpose of Clause 2(3) is to oblige any claimant in respect of property damage to give credit for compensation which he may have received or be entitled to receive under a claim he has made on another source or sources relative to that damage. The most common instances will involve compensation recovered under comprehensive motor or household policies. Policyholders with these covers cannot be forced to claim under them but will normally wish to do so for their convenience. Furthermore legal liability for the accident will not affect that claim and the MIB excess of £175 (Clause 2(4)) will not apply. Where such a claim has been made successfully MIB will only be concerned with the claimant's uninsured losses, eg, any excess he may have under his own policy, or loss of use of his vehicle subject to legal liability and the MIB excess of £175.

6 WHERE THERE IS A POLICY

In cases where it is ascertained that there is in existence a policy issued in compliance with the Road Traffic Act 1972, the insurer will act as the agent of the Bureau even if entitled to repudiate liability under the policy and, subject to notice being given as provided for in Clause 5(1)(a)(ii), will handle claims within the terms of the Agreement.

In many cases, particularly where the vehicle was being used without the policyholder's authority, the provisions of the Road Traffic Act precludes repudiation by the insurer of a victim's claim. Victims and those acting on their behalf are expressly reminded of the requirements as to the giving of notice to the insurer if the protection afforded to third parties by section 149 of the Road Traffic Act 1972 is sought. It must be stressed that the above arrangements are without prejudice to any rights insurers may have against their policyholders and, to avoid any possible misunderstanding, it is emphasised that there is nothing in this Agreement affecting any obligations imposed on a policyholder by his policy. Policyholders are not released from their contractual obligations to their insurers, although the Road Traffic Act and MIB protect THIRD PARTY VICTIMS from the consequences of failure to observe them. For example, if a policyholder fails to notify claims to his insurers as required by his policy or permits an unauthorised person to drive, he may be liable to his insurers.

WHERE THERE IS NO POLICY OR THE IDENTITY OF THE INSURER CANNOT BE ASCERTAINED

In cases where there is no policy, or for any reason the existence of a policy is in doubt or where there is a policy but the identity of the insurer cannot be ascertained, the victim or those acting on his behalf must notify the Bureau, and in practice it is desirable to inform the Bureau in all cases where the name of the insurer is not speedily forthcoming.

It is a condition of the Bureau's liability that they should be given notification in writing (with relevant documents) within seven days after the commencement of proceedings against the alleged person liable. It should always be remembered that the requirement for notice of issue of proceedings under Clause 5(1)(a)(i) and (ii) must be complied with strictly. Notice should be given immediately on issue of the proceedings, and such notice must be accompanied by copies of the writ or summons.

Wherever possible MIB wishes to resolve any claim by negotiation and will deal with claims, by agreement with the claimant, under the pre-action Protocol set out in the Appendix.

7   Claims arising out of the issue of uninsured vehicles owned by or in the possession of the Crown will in the majority of cases be outside the scope of the Bureau's liability (see Clause 6 of the Agreement – Exceptions). In such cases the approach should be made to the responsible authority in the usual way. The same benefits in respect of compensation will normally be afforded by the Crown to the victims in such cases as they would receive were the accident caused by a private vehicle, except where the victim is a serviceman or servicewoman whose death or injury gives rise to an entitlement to a pension or other compensation from public funds.

8   The purpose of Clause 6(1)(c) is to relieve MIB of liability to meet judgments in respect of damage to property obtained by persons who have compensated the victim such as the victim's own insurers. Such insurers have the right to attempt to recoup their outlay by requiring an insured to lend his name to proceedings against the person responsible, but MIB will not meet such claims as the victim has already been compensated.

9   Claims for damage to a vehicle or for losses arising therefrom for which a policy of insurance issued in compliance with Part IV of the Road Traffic Act 1972 is required, are excluded from the Agreement if the vehicle was not

insured and the claimant knew or ought to have known that it was not. See Clause 6(1)(d). The claim may also be excluded under Clause 6(1)(e).

10 It should be noted that the monetary limit applicable to property damage claims by virtue of Clause 2(2) corresponding with the insurance limit in section 145 of the Road Traffic Act 1972, and the excess prescribed by Clause 2(3) and (4) of this Agreement will be subject to review from time to time.

11 The Bureau have no liability UNDER THIS AGREEMENT to pay compensation in respect of any person who may suffer bodily injury or death or may sustain damage to property resulting from the use on a road of a vehicle, the owner or driver of which cannot be traced. A separate Agreement between the Secretary of State for Transport and the Bureau for the Compensation of Victims of Untraced Drivers in respect of bodily injury applies, but this Agreement does NOT embrace damage to property. (Copies of this Agreement may be obtained through Her Majesty's Stationery Office price £1.70.)

© *The Stationery Office. This material has been reproduced faithfully from material provided on MIB's website, though palpable errors have been amended.*

THE UNTRACED DRIVERS AGREEMENT 1996

14th June 1996

DEPARTMENT OF TRANSPORT

MOTOR INSURERS' BUREAU
(COMPENSATION OF VICTIMS OF
UNTRACED DRIVERS)

Text of an Agreement dated the 14 June 1996 between the Secretary of State for Transport and Motor Insurers' Bureau together with some notes on its scope and purpose.

THE AGREEMENT
RECITALS

1 On 21 April 1969 the Minister of Transport and Motor Insurers' Bureau entered into an Agreement ('the First Agreement') to secure compensation for Third party victims of road accidents when the driver responsible for the accident could not be traced.

2 The First Agreement was replaced by a new Agreement ('the Second Agreement') which operated in respect of accidents occurring on or after 1 December 1972.

3 The Second Agreement was added to by a Supplemental Agreement dated 7 December 1977 ('the Third Agreement') which operated in respect of accidents occurring on or after 3 January 1978.

4 The Second Agreement and the Third Agreement have now been replaced by a new Agreement ('this Agreement') which operates in respect of accidents occurring on or after 1 July 1996.

5 The text of this Agreement is as follows:

TEXT OF THE AGREEMENT

AN AGREEMENT made the 14th day of June 1996 between the Secretary of State for Transport ('the Secretary of State') and the Motor Insurers' Bureau, whose registered office is at 152 Silbury Boulevard, Milton Keynes, MK9 1NB ('the MIB').

IT IS HEREBY AGREED as follows:

1.1 Subject to paragraph (2) of this Clause, this Agreement applies to any case in which an Application is made to the MIB for a payment in respect of the death of or bodily injury to any person caused by or arising out of the use of a motor vehicle on a road in Great Britain and the case is one in which the following conditions are fulfilled, that is to say –

(a) the event giving rise to the death or injury occurred on or after 1 July 1996;

(b) the applicant for the payment either:

    (i) is unable to trace any person responsible for the death or injury, or

    (ii) in a case to which Clause 5 applies where more than one person was responsible, is unable to trace one of those persons;
    (any person so untraced is referred to as 'the untraced person');

(c) the death or injury was caused in such circumstances that on the balance of probabilities the untraced person would be liable to pay damages to the applicant in respect of the death or injury;

(d) the liability of the untraced person to pay damages to the applicant is one which is required to be covered by insurance or security under Part VI of the Road Traffic Act 1988 ('the 1988 Act'), it being assumed for this purpose, in the absence of evidence to the contrary, that the vehicle was being used in circumstances in which the user was required by the 1988 Act to be insured or secured against third party risks;

(e) the death or injury was not caused by the use of the vehicle by the untraced person in any deliberate attempt to cause the death or injury of the person in respect of which an application is made; and

(f) the application is made in writing within three years from the date of the event giving rise to the death or injury;

(g) the incident was reported to the police within 14 days or as soon as the applicant reasonably could and the applicant co-operated with the police.

1.2 This Agreement does not apply to a case in which –

(a) the death or bodily injury in respect of which any such application is made was caused by or arose out of the use of a motor vehicle which at the time of the event giving rise to the death or bodily injury was owned by or in the possession of the Crown, unless the case is one in which some other person has undertaken responsibility for the existence of a contract of insurance under the 1988 Act.

(b) at the time of the accident the person suffering death or bodily injury in respect of which the application is made was allowing himself to be carried in a vehicle and either before or after the commencement of his journey in the vehicle, if he could reasonably be expected to have alighted from the vehicle, he knew or had reason to believe that the vehicle:

(i) had been stolen or unlawfully taken; or

(ii) was being used without there being in force in relation to its use a contract of insurance which complied with the 1988 Act; or

(iii) was being used in the course or furtherance of crime; or

(iv) was being used as a means of escape from or avoidance of lawful apprehension.

1.3 For the purpose of paragraph (2) of this Clause –

(a) a vehicle which has been unlawfully removed from the possession of the Crown shall be taken to continue in that possession whilst it is kept so removed;

(b) references to a person being carried in a vehicle include references to his being carried in or upon, or entering or getting on to or alighting from the vehicle;

(c) 'owner' in relation to a vehicle which is the subject of a hiring agreement or a hire purchase agreement means the person in possession of the vehicle under that agreement.

2.1 An application to the MIB for a payment in respect of the death or bodily injury to any person may be made:

(a) by the person for whose benefit that payment is to be made ('the applicant'); or

(b) by any solicitor acting for the applicant; or

(c) by any other person whom the MIB may be prepared to accept as acting for the applicant.

2.2 Any decision made, or award or payment given or made or other thing done in accordance with this Agreement to or by a person acting under paragraph (1)(b) and (1)(c) of this Clause on behalf of the applicant, or in relation to an application made by such a person, shall, whatever may be the age, or the circumstances affecting the capacity, of the applicant, be treated as having the same effect as if it had been done to or by, or in relation to an application made by, an applicant of full age and capacity.

3 Subject to the following provisions of this Agreement, the MIB shall, on any application made to it in a case to which this Agreement applies, award to the applicant in respect of the death or injury for which the application is made a payment of an amount which shall be assessed in like manner as a court, applying English law in a case where the event giving rise to the death or injury occurred in England or Wales or applying the law of Scotland in a case where that event occurred in Scotland, would assess the damages which the applicant would have been entitled to recover from the untraced person in respect of that death or injury if the applicant had brought successful proceedings to enforce a claim for such damages against the untraced person.

4 In assessing the level of an award in accordance with Clause 3, the MIB shall be under no obligation to include in such award any sum in respect of loss of earnings suffered by the applicant where and in so far as the applicant has in fact been paid wages or salary or any sum in lieu of the same, whether or not such payments were made subject to an undertaking on the part of the applicant to repay the same in the event of the applicant recovering damages.

5.1 This Clause applies to any case:

(a) to which this Agreement applies; and

(b) the death or bodily injury in respect of which an application has been made to the MIB under this Agreement ('the relevant death or injury') was caused:

(i) partly by the untraced person and partly by an identified person, or by identified persons; or

(ii) partly by the untraced person and partly by some other untraced person or persons whose master or principal can be identified; and

(c) in circumstances making the identified person or persons or any master or principal ('the identified person') liable to the applicant in respect of the relevant death or injury.

5.2 If in a case to which this Clause applies one or other of the conditions in paragraph (3) of this Clause is satisfied, the amount of the award to be paid by the MIB to the applicant in respect of the relevant death or injury shall be determined in accordance with paragraph (4) of this Clause and its liability to the applicant shall be subject to paragraph (7) of this Clause and Clause 6 of this Agreement.

5.3 The conditions referred to in paragraph (2) of this Clause are:

(a) that the applicant has obtained a judgment in respect of the relevant death or injury against the identified person ('the original judgment') which has not been satisfied in full within three months from the date on which the applicant became entitled to enforce it ('the three month period'); or

(b) that the applicant –

(i) has not obtained and has not been required by the MIB to obtain a judgment in respect of the relevant death or injury against the identified person, and

(ii) has not received any payment by way of compensation from the identified person or persons.

5.4 The amount to be awarded by the MIB to the applicant in a case to which this Clause applies shall be determined as follows –

(a) if the condition in paragraph (3)(a) of this Clause is satisfied and the original judgment is wholly unsatisfied within the three month period, the amount to be awarded shall be an amount equal to that proportion of a full award attributable to the untraced person;

(b) if the condition in paragraph (3)(a) of this Clause is satisfied but the original judgment is satisfied in part only within the three month period, the amount to be awarded –

    (i) if the unsatisfied part of the original judgment is less than the proportion of a full award attributable to the untraced person, shall be an amount equal to that unsatisfied part, or

    (ii) if the unsatisfied part of the original judgment is equal to or greater than the proportion of a full award attributable to the untraced person, shall be an amount equal to the untraced person's proportion;

(c) if the condition in paragraph (3)(b) of this Clause is satisfied the amount to be awarded shall be an amount equal to the proportion of a full award attributable to the untraced person.

5.5 The following provisions of this paragraph shall have effect in any case in which an appeal from or any proceeding to set aside the original judgment is commenced within a period of three months beginning on the date on which the applicant became entitled to enforce the original judgment –

(a) until the said appeal or proceeding is disposed of the provisions of this Clause shall have effect as if for the three month period there were substituted a period expiring on the date when the said appeal or proceeding is disposed of;

(b) if as a result of the appeal or proceeding the applicant ceases to be entitled to receive any payment in respect of the relevant death or injury from any person or persons against whom he has obtained the original judgment the provisions of this Clause shall have effect as if he had neither obtained nor been required by the MIB to obtain a judgment against any person or persons;

(c) if as a result of the appeal or proceeding, the applicant becomes entitled to recover an amount which differs from that which he was entitled to recover under the original judgment, the provisions of this Clause shall have effect as if for the reference in paragraph (3)(a) to the original judgment there were substituted a reference to the judgment under which the applicant became entitled to the said different amount;

(d) if as a result of the said appeal or proceeding the applicant remains entitled to enforce the original judgment the provisions of this Clause shall have effect as if for the three month period there were substituted a period of three months beginning on the date on which the appeal or other proceeding was disposed of.

The provisions of this paragraph shall apply also in any case where any judgment given upon any such appeal or proceeding is itself the subject of a further appeal or similar proceeding and shall apply in such a case in relation to that further appeal or proceeding in the same manner as they apply in relation to the first mentioned appeal or proceeding.

5.6   In this Clause –

(a) 'full award' means the amount which would have fallen to be awarded to the applicant under Clause 3 in respect of the relevant death or injury if the untraced person had been adjudged by a court to be wholly responsible for that death or injury; and

(b) 'the proportion of a full award attributable to the untraced person' means that proportion of a full award which on the balance of probabilities would have been apportioned by a court in proceedings between the untraced person and any other person liable in respect of the same event as the share to be borne by the untraced person in the responsibility for the event giving rise to the relevant death or injury.

5.7   The MIB shall not be under any liability in respect of the relevant death or injury if the applicant is entitled to receive compensation from the MIB in respect of that death or injury under any Agreement providing for the compensation of victims of uninsured drivers entered into between the Secretary of State and the MIB.

6.1   Any liability falling upon the MIB upon an application made to it under this Agreement in respect of any death or injury, shall be subject to the following conditions:

(a) the applicant shall give all such assistance as may reasonably be required by or on behalf of the MIB to enable any investigation to be carried out under this Agreement, including, in particular, the provision of statements and information either in writing, or, if so required, orally at an interview or interviews between the applicant and any person acting on behalf of the MIB;

(b) at any time before the MIB has communicated its decision upon the application to the applicant, the applicant shall, subject to the following provisions of this Clause, take all such steps as in the circumstances it is reasonable for the MIB to require him to take to obtain judgment against any person or persons in respect of their liability to the applicant for the death or injury as having caused or contributed to that death or injury or as being the master or principal of any person who has caused or contributed to that death or injury; and

(c) if required by the MIB the applicant shall assign to the MIB or to its nominee any judgment obtained by him (whether or not obtained in accordance with a requirement under subparagraph (b) of this paragraph) in respect of the death or injury to which his application to the MIB relates upon such terms as will secure that the MIB or its nominee shall be accountable to the applicant for any amount by which the aggregate of all sums recovered by the MIB or its nominee under the judgment (after deducting all reasonable expenses incurred in effecting such recovery) exceeds the amount payable by the MIB to the applicant under this Agreement in respect of that death or injury.

6.2 If the MIB requires the applicant to bring proceedings against any specified person or persons –

(a) the MIB shall indemnify the applicant against all costs reasonably incurred by him in complying with that requirement unless the result of those proceedings materially contributes to establishing that the untraced person did not cause or contribute to the relevant death or injury; and

(b) the applicant shall, if required by the MIB and at its expense, provide the MIB with a transcript of any official shorthand note taken in those proceedings of any evidence given or judgment delivered therein.

6.3 In the event of a dispute arising between the applicant and the MIB as to the reasonableness of any requirement by the MIB under paragraph (1)(b) of this Clause or as to whether any such costs as are referred to in paragraph (2)(a) of this Clause were reasonably incurred, that dispute shall be referred to the Secretary of State whose decision shall be final.

Provided that any dispute arising between the applicant and the MIB as to whether the MIB are required to indemnify him under paragraph (2)(a) of this Clause shall, in so far as it depends on the question whether the result of any proceedings which the MIB has required the applicant to bring against any specified person or persons has or has not materially contributed to establish that the untraced person did not cause or contribute to the relevant death or injury, be referred to the arbitrator in accordance with the following provisions of this Agreement, whose decision on that question shall be final.

7 The MIB shall cause any application made to it for a payment under this Agreement to be investigated and, unless it decides that the application should be rejected because a preliminary investigation has disclosed that the case is not one to which this Agreement applies, it shall cause a report to be made on the application and on the basis of that report it shall decide whether to make an award and, if so, the amount of the award which shall be calculated in accordance with the provisions of this Agreement.

8 The MIB may before coming to a decision on any application made to it under this Agreement request the applicant to provide it with a statutory declaration to be made by the applicant, setting out to the best of his knowledge, information and belief the facts and circumstances upon which his claim to an award under this Agreement are based, or facts and circumstances as may be specified by it.

9.1 The MIB shall notify its decision to the applicant and when so doing shall –

(a) if the application is rejected because a preliminary investigation has disclosed that it is not one made in a case to which this Agreement applies, give its reasons for the rejection; or

(b) if the application has been fully investigated provide him with a statement setting out:

(i) the circumstances in which the death or injury occurred and the relevant evidence,

(ii) the circumstances relevant to the assessment of the amount to be awarded to the applicant under this Agreement and the relevant evidence, and

(iii) if it refuses to make an award, its reasons for that refusal; and

(c) in a case to which Clause 5 of this Agreement applies specify the way in which the amount of that award has been computed and its relation to those provisions of Clause 5 which are relevant to its computation.

9.2 Where the MIB has decided that it will not indemnify the applicant against the costs of any proceedings which it has under Clause 6(1)(b) required him to bring against any specified person or persons on the ground that those proceedings have materially contributed to establish that the untraced person did not cause or contribute to the relevant death or injury, it shall give notice to the applicant of that decision together with its reasons for it and shall provide the applicant with a copy of any transcript of any evidence given or judgment delivered in those proceedings as is mentioned in Clause 6(2)(b) hereof which it regards as relevant to that decision.

10.1 Subject to the provisions of this Agreement, where the MIB has decided to make an award to the applicant, it shall pay the applicant the amount of that award if:

(a) it has been notified by the applicant that the award is accepted; or

(b) at the expiration of the period during which the applicant may give notice of an appeal under Clause 11 the applicant has not given the MIB either any such notification of the acceptance of its award or a notice of an appeal under Clause 11.

10.2 Such payment as is made under paragraph (1) of this Clause shall discharge the MIB from all liability under this Agreement in respect of the death or injury for which that award has been made.

11.1 The applicant shall have a right of appeal to an arbitrator against any decision notified to him by the MIB under Clause 9 if:

(a) he gives notice to the MIB, that he wishes to appeal against its decision ('the notice of appeal');

(b) he gives the MIB the notice of appeal within 6 weeks from the date when he was given notice of the decision against which he wishes to appeal; and

(c) he has not previously notified the MIB that he has accepted its decision.

11.2 The grounds of appeal are as follows:

(a) where the application has not been the subject of a full investigation:

    (i) that the case is one to which this Agreement applies, and

    (ii) that the applicant's application should be fully investigated by the MIB with a view to its deciding whether or not to make an award to him and, if so, the amount of that award; or

(b) where the application has been fully investigated:

    (i) that the MIB was wrong in refusing to make an award, or

    (ii) that the amount it has awarded to the applicant is insufficient; or

(c) in a case where a decision not to indemnify the applicant against the costs of any proceedings has been notified to the applicant by the MIB under Clause 9.2, that that decision was wrong.

12 A notice of appeal under Clause 11 shall state the grounds of the appeal and shall be accompanied by an undertaking given by the applicant or by the person acting on his behalf under Clause 2(1)(b) and 2(1)(c), that –

(a) the applicant will accept the decision of the arbitrator; and

(b) the arbitrator's fee shall be paid to the MIB by the applicant or by the person who has given the undertaking in any case where the MIB is entitled to reimbursement of that fee under the provisions of Clause 22.

13.1 When giving notice of his appeal or at any time before doing so, the applicant may:

(a) make comments to the MIB on its decision; and

(b) supply it with such particulars as he thinks fit of any further evidence not contained in the written statement supplied to him by the MIB which he considers is relevant to the application.

13.2 The MIB may, before submitting the applicant's appeal to the arbitrator:

(a) cause an investigation to be made into the further evidence supplied by the applicant under paragraph (1)(b) of this Clause; and

(b) report to the applicant the result of that investigation and of any change in its decision which may result from it.

13.3 The applicant may, within six weeks from the date on which the report referred to in paragraph (2)(b) of this Clause was sent to him, unless he withdraws his appeal, make such comments on the report as he may desire to have submitted to the arbitrator.

14.1 In a case where the MIB receives from the applicant a notice of appeal in which the only ground of appeal which is stated is that the amount awarded to the applicant is insufficient, before submitting that appeal to the arbitrator the MIB may:

(a) give notice to the applicant that if the appeal proceeds it will request the arbitrator to decide whether the case is one in which the MIB should make an award at all; and

(b) at the same time as complying with paragraph (1)(a) of this Clause provide the applicant with a statement setting out such comments as it may consider relevant to the decision which the arbitrator should come to on that question.

14.2 Where the MIB gives the applicant notice under paragraph (1)(a) of this Clause, the applicant may, within six weeks from the date on which that notice is given:

(a) make such comments to the MIB and supply it with particulars of other evidence not contained in any written statement provided to him by the MIB as he may consider relevant to the question which the arbitrator is by that notice requested to decide; and

(b) Clause 13 shall apply in relation to any comments made or particulars supplied by the applicant under paragraph (2)(a) of this Clause.

15.1 Subject to paragraph (2) of this Clause, where the MIB receives a notice of appeal from the applicant under the provisions of this Agreement, unless the appeal is previously withdrawn, it shall:

(a) submit that appeal to an arbitrator for a decision; and

(b) send to the arbitrator for the purpose of obtaining his decision:

   (i) the application made by the applicant;

   (ii) a copy of its decision as notified to the applicant; and

   (iii) copies of all statements, declarations, notices, undertakings, comments, transcripts, particulars of reports provided, given or sent to the MIB under this Agreement either by the applicant or any person acting for him under Clause 2(1)(b) or 2(1)(c) by the MIB.

15.2 In a case where the MIB causes an investigation to be made under Clause 13, the MIB shall not comply with paragraph (1) of this Clause until:

(a) the expiration of six weeks from the date on which it sent the applicant a report as to the result of that investigation; or

(b) the expiration of six weeks from the date on which it gave the applicant notice under Clause 14(1); or

(c) the expiration of six weeks from the date on which it sent the applicant a report as to the result of that investigation, if it has caused an investigation to be made into any evidence supplied under Clause 14(2).

16 On an appeal made by the applicant in accordance with this Agreement:

(a) if the appeal is against a decision by the MIB rejecting an application because a preliminary investigation has disclosed that the case is not one to which this Agreement applies, the arbitrator shall decide whether the case is or is not one to which this Agreement applies and, if he decides that it is such a case, shall remit the application to the MIB for full investigation and a decision in accordance with the provisions of this Agreement;

(b) if the appeal is against a decision by the MIB given after an application has been fully investigated by it (whether before the appeal or in consequence of its being remitted for such investigation under paragraph (a) of this Clause) the arbitrator shall decide, as may be appropriate, having regard to the grounds stated in the notice of appeal and to any notice given by the MIB to the applicant under Clause 14, whether the MIB should make an award under this Agreement to the applicant and, if so, the amount which it should award to the applicant under the provisions of this Agreement;

(c) if the appeal relates to a dispute which has arisen between the applicant and the MIB which is required by the proviso to Clause 6(3) to be referred to the arbitrator, the arbitrator shall also give his decision on that dispute.

Provided that where the arbitrator has allowed an appeal under paragraph (a) of this Clause all the provisions of this Agreement shall apply as if the case were an application to which this Agreement applies upon which the MIB had not communicated a decision.

17.1 Subject to paragraph (2) of this Clause, the arbitrator shall decide the appeal on the documents submitted to him under Clause 15(1)(b) and no further evidence shall be produced to him.

17.2 The following shall apply where documents have been submitted to the arbitrator under Clause 15(1)(b):

(a) the arbitrator shall be entitled to ask the MIB to make any further investigation which he considers desirable and to submit a written report of its findings to him for his consideration; and

(b) the MIB shall send a copy of that report to the applicant who shall be entitled to submit written comments on it to the MIB within four weeks of the date on which that copy is sent to him; and

(c) the MIB shall transmit those comments to the arbitrator for his consideration.

18 The arbitrator by whom an appeal made by an applicant in accordance with the provisions of this Agreement shall be considered shall be an arbitrator to be selected by the Secretary of State from two panels of Queen's Counsel appointed respectively by the Lord Chancellor and the Lord Advocate for the purpose of determining appeals under this Agreement, the arbitrator to be selected from the panel appointed by the Lord Chancellor in cases where the event giving rise to the death or injury occurred in England or Wales and from the panel appointed by the Lord Advocate where that event occurred in Scotland.

19 The arbitrator shall notify his decision on any appeal under this Agreement to the MIB and the MIB shall forthwith send a copy of the Arbitrator's decision to the applicant.

20 Subject to the provisions of this Agreement, the MIB shall pay the applicant any amount which the arbitrator has decided shall be awarded to him, and that payment shall discharge the MIB from all liability under this Agreement in respect of the death or injury in respect of which that decision has been given.

21 Each party to the appeal will bear their own costs.

22 The MIB shall pay the arbitrator a fee approved by the Lord Chancellor or the Lord Advocate, as the case may be, after consultation with the MIB.

Provided that, in any case where it appears to the arbitrator that there were no reasonable grounds for the appeal, the arbitrator may in his discretion decide:

(a) that his fee ought to be paid by the applicant; and

(b) that the person giving the undertaking required by Clause 12 shall be liable to reimburse the MIB the amount of the fee paid by it to the arbitrator, except in so far as that amount is deducted by the MIB from any amount which it is liable to pay to the applicant in consequence of the decision of the arbitrator.

23 If in any case it appears to the MIB that by reason of the applicant being under the age of majority or of any other circumstances affecting his capacity to manage his affairs it would be in the applicant's interest that all or some part of the amount which would otherwise be payable to him under an award made under this Agreement should be administered for him by the Family Welfare Association or by some other body or person under a trust or by the Court of Protection (or in Scotland by the appointment of a Judicial Factor) the MIB may establish for that purpose a trust of the whole or part of the amount to take effect for a period and under provisions as may appear to it to be appropriate in the circumstances of the case or may initiate or cause any other person to initiate process in that Court and otherwise cause any amount payable under the award to be paid to and administered thereby.

24 In any case in which an application has been made to the MIB under Clause 2.1 and in which a preliminary investigation under Clause 7 has disclosed that the case is one to which the Agreement, save for Clause 5, applies, the MIB may, instead of causing a report to be made on the application as provided by Clause 7, make, or cause to be made, to the applicant an offer to settle his application in a specified sum, assessed in accordance with Clause 3.

25 Where an offer is made under Clause 24, there shall be provided to the applicant (at the same time) in writing particulars of:

(a) the circumstances in which the death or injury occurred and the relevant evidence; and

(b) the circumstances relevant to the assessment of the amount to be awarded to the applicant and the relevant evidence.

26.1 On receipt by the MIB or its agent of an acceptance of the offer referred to in Clause 24:

(a) this acceptance shall have effect in relation to the application as if in Clause 7 the words 'and, unless the MIB decide' to the end of that Clause, and Clauses 9 to 22 inclusive were omitted; and

(b) the MIB shall pay to the applicant the amount specified in the offer.

26.2 The payment made by the MIB under paragraph (1)(b) of this Clause shall discharge it from all liability under this Agreement in respect of the death or injury for which the payment has been made.

27 This Agreement may be determined at any time by the Secretary of State or by the MIB by either of them giving to the other not less than 12 months' previous notice in writing.

Provided that this Agreement shall continue to have effect in any case where the event giving rise to the death or injury occurred before the date on which this Agreement terminates in accordance with any notice so given.

28 From 14 June 1996 the following periods of operation shall apply:

(a) this Agreement shall come into operation on 1 July 1996 in relation to accidents occurring on or after that date;

(b) the Second Agreement shall cease and determine except in relation to applications arising out of accidents which occurred on or after 1 December 1972 and before 3 January 1978; and

(c) the Third Agreement shall cease and determine except in relation to accidents occurring on or after 3 January 1978 and before the 1 July 1996.

IN WITNESS whereof the Secretary of State for Transport has caused his Corporate Seal to be hereto affixed and the Motor Insurers' Bureau has caused its Common Seal to be hereto affixed the day and year first above written.

THE CORPORATE SEAL of
the Secretary of State for Transport
hereunto affixed is authenticated by:

THE COMMON SEAL of
the Motor Insurers' Bureau
was hereunto affixed in the
presence of

Directors of the Board of Management
Secretary

NOTES

The following Notes are for the guidance of those who may wish to make application to the Motor Insurers' Bureau for payment under the Agreement, and for the guidance of their legal advisers, but they must not be taken as making unnecessary a careful study of the Agreement itself. Communications connected with the Agreement should be addressed to the Motor Insurers' Bureau ('the MIB'), whose address in 152 Silbury Boulevard, Central Milton Keynes, MK9 1NB.

1   This Agreement replaces a previous one dated 22nd November 1972 and a Supplemental Agreement dated 7th December 1977 and continues the arrangements which have existed since 1946 under which the MIB has made *ex gratia* payments in respect of death or personal injuries resulting from the use on the road of a motor vehicle the owner or driver of which cannot be traced. Provision is made for an appeal against the MIB's decision in such cases.

2   The Agreement dated 22nd November 1972 applies to a death or bodily injury arising out of an accident occurring on a road in Great Britain on or after 1st December 1972 and before 3rd January 1978. The Agreement dated 22nd November 1972 as supplemented by the Supplemental Agreement dated 7th January 1977 applies in relation to accidents occurring on or after 3rd January 1978 and before 1 July 1996. This Agreement applies in relation to accidents occurring on or after 1 July 1996.

3   Subject to the terms of the Agreement, the MIB will accept applications for a payment in respect of the death of, or bodily injury to any person resulting from the use of a motor vehicle on a road in Great Britain in any cases in which –

(a) the applicant for the payment cannot trace any person responsible for the death or injury (or, in certain circumstances, a person partly responsible) (Clause 1(1)(b)); and

(b) the death or injury was caused in such circumstances that the untraced person would be liable to pay damages to the applicant in respect of the death or injury (Clause 1(1)(c)); and

(c) the untraced person's liability to the applicant is one which at the time the accident occurred, was required to be covered by insurance or security (Clause 1(1)(d)).

The MIB will not deal with the following:

(a) deliberate 'running down' cases (Clause 1(1)(e));

(b) certain other cases relating to Crown vehicles; and

(c) certain categories of 'voluntary' passenger (Clause 1(2)–(4)).

4   Applications for a payment under the Agreement must be made in writing to the MIB within three years of the date of the accident giving rise to the death or injury (Clause 1(1)(f)).

5   Under Clause 3, the amount which the MIB will award will (except for the exclusion of those elements of damages mentioned in Clause 4) be assessed in the same way as a Court would have assessed the amount of damages payable by the untraced person had the applicant been able to bring a successful claim for damages against him.

6   Clause 5 relates to cases where an untraced person and an identified person are each partly responsible for a death or injury, and defines the conditions under which the MIB will in such cases make a contribution in respect of the responsibility of the untraced person.

7   Under Clause 6(1)(b), the MIB may require the applicant to bring proceedings against any identified person who may be responsible for the death or injury, subject to indemnifying the applicant as to his costs as provided in Clause 6(2) and 6(3).

8   On receipt of an application, the MIB will, if satisfied that the application comes within the terms of the Agreement, investigate the circumstances and, when this has been done, decide whether to make a payment and, if so, how much (Clause 7).

9   The MIB may request the applicant to make a statutory declaration setting out all, or some, of the facts on which his application is based (Clause 8).

10   The MIB may notify the applicant of its decision, setting out the circumstances of the case and the evidence on which it bases its decision and, if it refuses to make a payment, the reasons for the refusal (Clause 9).

11   If the applicant wishes to appeal against the decision on the grounds specified in Clause 11(2), he must notify the MIB within six weeks of being notified of the decision, and he or any person acting on his behalf shall give the undertakings set out in Clause 12.

12 The MIB may, as a result of the comments made and further evidence submitted by the applicant on its decision, investigate the further evidence, and if so it will communicate with the applicant again. In such a case the applicant will have six weeks from the date of that further communication in which to decide whether or not to go on with the appeal (Clause 13).

13 Where the applicant appeals only on the grounds that the amount awarded to him is too low, the MIB may give him notice that if the matter proceeds to appeal, it will ask the arbitrator to decide also the issue of the MIB's liability to make any payment. The applicant will have six weeks from the date of any such notice in which to comment to the MIB on this intention (Clause 14).

14 Appeals will be decided by an arbitrator who will be a Queen's Counsel selected by the Secretary of State for Transport from one of two panels to be appointed by the Lord Chancellor and the Lord Advocate respectively (Clause 18).

15 All appeals will be decided by the arbitrator on the basis of the relevant documents (as set out in Clause 15) which will be sent to him by the MIB. If the arbitrator asks the MIB to make a further investigation, the applicant will have an opportunity to comment on the result of that investigation (Clause 17).

16 The arbitrator may, at his discretion, award the cost of this fee against the applicant if he considers the appeal unreasonable; otherwise, each party to the appeal will bear their own costs, the MIB paying the arbitrator's fee (Clauses 21 and 22).

17 In certain circumstances, the MIB may establish a trust for the benefit of an applicant of the whole or part of any award (Clause 23).

18 Clauses 24 to 26 provide for the use of a shorter form of procedure than that stipulated in Clause 7 with the object of securing speedier disposal of certain applications to the MIB. The MIB may, at its discretion, make an offer of an award in a specified sum providing the applicant at the same time with particulars of the circumstances of the case and of the evidence on which the offer is based. If the applicant is prepared to accept the offer, thus undertaking, on payment by the MIB, to forgo any right of appeal to an arbitrator, the MIB will pay the sum offered forthwith. If the offer is not acceptable the application will thereafter be dealt with in accordance with the full procedure set out in the Agreement.

The shorter form of procedure does not apply in a case where both an untraced person and an identified person may each partly be responsible for injuries giving rise to an application to the MIB.

THE MOTOR ACCIDENT SOLICITORS SOCIETY

The Motor Accident Solicitors Society (MASS) promotes the highest standards of legal services through education and representation in the pursuit of justice for the victims of road traffic accidents.

For more information regarding membership contact the MASS office.

MASS office address:

The MASS Central Office
54 Baldwin Street
Bristol BS1 1QW

Tel: 0117 929 2560

Fax: 0117 904 7220

DX: 78156 Bristol

Email: office@mass.org.uk

INDEX